The HUGE Book of Amazing Facts & Interesting Stuff

2024

JENNY KELLETT

The HUGE Book of Amazing Facts and Interesting Stuff 2024

www.bellanovabooks.com

Contents

Introduction

Welcome to the special 10-year edition of "The HUGE Book of Amazing Facts and Interesting Stuff"! As we celebrate a decade of dedication to uncovering the most fascinating, curious, and mind-boggling facts, we reflect on the journey that has brought us here.

Since our first edition back in 2014, the world has witnessed a whirlwind of monumental events and transformations. We've seen the rise of groundbreaking technologies that have changed the way we communicate, work, and live. Social media has evolved from budding platforms to pivotal tools in shaping public opinion and driving social movements. Climate change has taken center stage, with increasing awareness and action aimed at preserving our planet for future generations. We've marveled at the advances in space exploration, celebrating humanity's indomitable spirit of discovery as we reached new frontiers beyond Earth's atmosphere.

The mid-2010s brought us moments of triumph and tragedy, innovation, and introspection, setting the stage for the tumultuous 2020s. From the war in Europe to the global pandemic that fundamentally altered our way of life, these years have been a testament to our resilience and our capacity for adaptation.

As a writer, the last decade has been equally as defining for me. What started as a fun project when I started scribbling fun facts in my notebook on the train to work as a journalist, has evolved into a full-time career.

Growing up, I was obsessed with facts—I couldn't consume enough of them. I would go to sleep with an almanac or the Guinness Book of Records under my pillow, and could whip out a fun fact about almost any topic on demand (although usually without anyone asking for it!).

While I have now published dozens of non-fiction books, this particular one has a special place in my heart. Every February, after the craziness of Christmas festivities has died down, I lock myself away to dive deep into the depths of the internet to find the best moments of the past 12 months.

Thank you for being on this journey with me—whether this is your first purchase, or you've been here since the start.

Now, prepare to be enthralled, educated, and inspired. Welcome to "The HUGE Book of Amazing Facts and Interesting Stuff 2024".

Then & Now

For this anniversary edition, I thought it'd be fun to look back on the last 10 years and see what has changed—in numbers. Amongst all the bad news that is currently dominating our screens, it's great to see some positive changes thrown in there too.

All facts are based on the closest reliable data, in 2023 where possible.

THEN &NOW

Global Internet Usage

Then (2014): Approximately 2.7 billion people were using the internet, about 40% of the world's population.

Now (2024): Internet users have grown to over 5 billion, accounting for more than 60% of the global population. In 2023 alone, 97 million users came online for the first time.

Renewable Energy Usage

Then (2014): Global renewable energy accounted for approximately 13.8% of total global energy production.

Now (2024): In 2023, renewable electricity capacity soared to an estimated 507 GW, marking a nearly 50% increase from the previous year. It currently stands at around 30% of global energy production.

Protected Natural Areas

Then (2014): 15.4% of terrestrial and inland water areas were protected.

Now (2024): Over 17% of such areas are now under protection, aiming to preserve biodiversity. The goal is to reach 30% by 2030.

Global Literacy Rates

Then (2014): The global adult literacy rate was about 85%.

Now (2024): It has risen to approximately 87%, with some regions experiencing more significant gains. The average literacy rate of most developed countries is 99%.

Electric Vehicle (EV) Sales

Then (2014): Global sales of electric vehicles were just over 350,000.

Now (2024): Sales have skyrocketed as EV technology has advanced and become more affordable. A total of 14.2 million EV's were sold in 2023.

Population of Endangered Tigers

Then (2014): The wild tiger population was estimated at around 3,500.

Now (2024): Conservation efforts have helped tiger increase numbers to around 5,574 in late 2023.

Space Exploration

Then (2014): The Voyager 1 spacecraft had recently entered interstellar space, about 19 billion kilometers from Earth.

Now (2024): Voyager 1 is over 24 billion kilometers away, and several new interplanetary missions have been launched, including a planned manned mission to Mars in the 2030s.

Social Media Presence

Then (2014): Facebook had about 1.39 billion active monthly users.

Now (2024): Facebook's user numbers have grown to over three billion. Meanwhile, platforms like TikTok, which didn't exist in 2014, have rapidly grown to boast 1.56 billion users.

World Health

Then (2014): The average global life expectancy was around 71 years.

Now (2024): Life expectancy has increased to about 73 years, despite the setbacks from the pandemic.

Global Population

Then (2014): The world's population was around 7.2 billion.

Now (2024): It has increased to approximately 8.1 billion. The early 19th century marked the moment when the global population first hit one billion. Today, we experience an increase of one billion people approximately every 12 to 15 years.

Deforestation in the Amazon

Then (2014): The Brazilian Amazon saw approximately 4,848 square kilometers of deforestation.

Now (2024): By 2023, significant efforts led to a reduction, with satellite monitoring detecting 5,152 square kilometers of forest cover destroyed, down 50 percent from 2022. Despite this significant yearly reduction, the deforestation extent in 2023 remains closely comparable to the 2014 figure.

Global Artificial Intelligence Market

Then (2014): In 2014, the global AI market was valued at approximately $6.3 billion.

Now (2024): By 2023, it expanded significantly to $150.2 billion and is projected to continue growing at a rate of 36.8% (CAGR), reaching around $1,345.2 billion by 2030.

Global Mobile Phone Usage

Then (2014): There were about 6.9 billion mobile phone subscriptions worldwide.

Now (2024): The number has exceeded 8.9 billion, with smartphones accounting for a large majority.

Homicide Rates in the USA

Then (2014): The homicide rate in the USA was 4.5 per 100,000 people, with the state of Louisiana having the highest rate in the country.

Now (2024): Despite homicide rates peaking to 6.81 per 100,000 people during the Covid pandemic, 2023 saw a drastic drop of around 12%.

Worldwide Internet Speeds

Then (2014): The global average internet connection speed was around 4.5 Mbps.

Now (2024): The average speed has increased multifold to 46.8 Mbps, with many areas now having access to gigabit connections.

Space Debris

Then (2014): There were an estimated 16,000 tracked pieces of space debris.

Now (2024): With the increase in satellite launches, space debris has become a critical issue, with around 35,150 pieces being tracked and initiatives underway to address the problem. There are an estimated 130 million untracked pieces of space debris.

Public Electric Vehicle Charging Stations

Then (2014): There were around 100,000 public charging stations for electric vehicles worldwide.

Now (2024): The infrastructure has expanded massively, with over 2.7 million charging points available globally at the end of 2022.

Wind Energy Generation

Then (2014): Global wind energy capacity was about 153.4 billion kWh, or 2.78% of total energy generation.

Now (2024): Capacity has more than doubled, with wind energy capacity reaching 1 Terawatt.

Plastic Waste Production

Then (2014): Approximately 311 million tonnes of plastic waste were produced.

Now (2024): Plastic waste generation has increased to over 400 million tonnes, but so have recycling rates and initiatives to reduce single-use plastics.

Number of Cryptocurrency Users

Then (2014): Cryptocurrency was still a niche market with a few million users. In 2016, there were 5 million users.

Now (2024): The user base has exploded, with over 425 million cryptocurrency users worldwide.

World Heritage Sites

Then (2014): There were 1,007 UNESCO World Heritage Sites.

Now (2024): The list has expanded to include more sites that are of cultural, historical, or scientific significance. As of September 2023 there are 1,199 UNESCO World Heritage Sites.

Annual CO2 Emissions

Then (2014): Global CO2 emissions were about 32.3 billion tonnes.

Now (2024): Global CO2 emissions reached a record high of 37.4 billion tonnes in 2023—a 1.1% increase on the previous year.

Global Unemployment Rate

Then (2014): The global unemployment rate was estimated at 5.6%.

Now (2024): The job market has experienced fluctuations, especially post-pandemic, but there's a trend towards recovery and a shift in the types of employment that are in demand. It currently sits at 5.1%.

Global Average Sea Level Rise

Then (2014): Average sea levels had risen by about 3 inches (7.62 cm) since 1993.

Now (2024): Global average sea level rose by about 0.3 inches (0.76 cm) from 2022 to 2023, which is 4 inches (9.4 cm) more than in 1993.

Human Genome Sequencing Cost

Then (2014): The cost to sequence a human genome was just under $1,000.

Now (2024): Advances in genomics have reduced the cost to around $600.

Global VR Market Size

Then (2014): In 2014, the global market for virtual and augmented reality was nearly $4.5 billion.

Now (2024): By 2023, the market was projected to reach $142.4 billion.

Petrol Prices

Then (2014): In the UK, the average cost of unleaded petrol in 2014 was around £1.27 per litre, while diesel was around £1.34 per litre.

Now (2024): As of April 2024, the average price for petrol was £1.46 and £1.53 for diesel.

Number of Known Exoplanets

Then (2014): About 1,800 exoplanets had been identified.

Now (2024): The number of confirmed exoplanets has skyrocketed, now numbering over 5,500, with many more candidates being studied. There has been a huge increase in exoplanet discoveries since 2014 thanks to the powerful Kepfler spacecraft.

Global Malaria Cases

Then (2014): There were an estimated 198 million cases of malaria worldwide.

Now (2024): In 2023, the global number of malaria cases was reported to have reached 249 million. This represents a significant increase from the estimated number of cases before the COVID-19 pandemic, and an uptick of five million cases over the previous year.

Worldwide Smartphone Penetration

Then (2014): Around 22% of people globally had a smartphone.

Now (2024): In 2022 (the latest data), the global smartphone penetration rate was estimated at 68%.

Average Global Temperatures

Then (2014): The average global temperature was about 0.74°C above the 20th-century average.

Now (2024): By 2023, this had significantly increased, with the average global temperature for the year reaching 1.18°C above the 20th-century average, marking it as the warmest year on record since global records began in 1850.

Data Created Daily

Then (2014): About 2.5 quintillion bytes of data were generated each day (that's 2.5 followed by 18 zeros!).

Now (2024): The amount of data generated daily has grown exponentially, now estimated at over 3.2 quintillion bytes every hour.

Online Learning USA

Then (2014): In 2014, around 6 million students in the U.S. were enrolled in at least one online course, representing over 30% of all students.

Now (2024): In the fall of 2021 (latest available data), around 9.4 million U.S. undergraduate students, or 61% of all undergraduates, were enrolled in at least one distance education course.

Terrorism Impact

Then (2014): In 2014, there were an estimated 12,000 deaths from terrorism worldwide, a 61% increase from 2013.

Now (2024): In 2023, there were 8,352 deaths from terrorism, a 22% increase from 2022 but still 23% lower than the peak in 2015.

Growth of Telemedicine

Then (2014): In 2014, the global mHealth (mobile health) market, which includes telemedicine, was valued at around $6.7 billion.

Now (2024): By 2023, the global telemedicine market was valued at nearly $115 billion, and is projected to reach $286 billion by 2030.

Conservation Status of Species

Then (2014): The IUCN Red List contained over 11,200 species threatened with extinction.

Now (2024): The list now contains over 44,000 species threatened with extinction. However, tens of thousands of new species have been assessed, so a truly accurate figure is not available. Several species, such as the Iberian lynx and the Guadalupe fur seal have successfully been moved off the list over the past decade.

Growth of Online Shopping

Then (2014): E-commerce sales were roughly $1.3 trillion globally.

Now (2024): Online shopping has become the norm for many consumers, with global e-commerce sales exceeding $5.8 trillion in 2023.

Cybersecurity Threats

Then (2014): It was estimated that cybercrime cost the world between $345 billion and $445 billion.

Now (2024): Cybercrime is predicted to cost the world $9.5 trillion USD in 2024.

Book Publishing Revenue

Then (2014): The global revenue for book publishers was around $114 billion.

Now (2024): The global book publishing revenue was expected to reach an estimated $132.4 billion in 2023.

E-books vs. Print Books Sales

Then (2014): E-books were gaining ground, accounting for about 25% of the total book market in the US.

Now (2024): Print has experienced a resurgence, known as the 'print renaissance', with e-book sales stabilising. Ebooks now account for 6.94% of total publishing industry revenue in the US.

Netflix Subscribers

Then (2014): Netflix had 57.4 million subscribers globally.

Now (2024): Netflix and other streaming services have seen massive subscriber growth, with Netflix alone boasting over 260 million subscribers at the end of 2023.

North American Box Office Revenue

Then (2014): In 2014, the North American box office revenue reached an estimated $10.4 billion.

Now (2024): The North American box office is estimated to have reached $9.07 billion in 2023, up 21% from 2022 but still 21% behind the 2017-2019 pre-pandemic average.

Average Movie Ticket Price

Then (2014): In 2014, the average movie ticket in the USA cost $8.17.

Now (2024): In 2024, the average movie ticket costs $10.78 (not adjusted for inflation).

Music Streaming Revenue

Then (2014): The total revenue of music streaming services was around $1.87 billion.

Now (2024): As streaming has become the predominant form of music consumption, revenues have surged to over $13 billion.

Podcast Listenership

Then (2014): Podcasting was a growing trend with a listener base of about 39 million North Americans per month.

Now (2024): Podcasts have become mainstream, with over 149.4 million North Americans listeners per month. Global listenership is expected to reach 504.9 million in 2024.

Video Game Industry Revenue

Then (2014): The global video game market was worth about $93 billion.

Now (2024): The industry has seen tremendous growth, with market value surpassing $180 billion, buoyed by mobile gaming and the rise of esports.

The Rise of Audiobooks

Then (2014): Audiobook sales revenue in the United States reached $871 million in the first part of 2014, up 7.5% from the same period in 2013.

Now (2024): Audiobooks have seen exponential growth, becoming a multi-billion-dollar industry. In 2022, audiobook sales revenue in the United States reached an estimated $1.8 billion.

Average Cost of a Gallon of Milk

Then (2014): The average cost was around $3.52 in the United States.

Now (2024): In January 2024, the average price for a gallon of whole milk was $3.958.

Number of Scripted TV Shows

Then (2014): There were around 376 scripted original series on American television.

Now (2024): The number of scripted shows has exploded, with streaming services contributing significantly to a "golden age" of television content. However, in 2023, the number of US original scripted TV series declined 14% to 516, down from 600 in 2022, largely due to Hollywood strikes.

Theatre Attendance on Broadway

Then (2014): In 2014, Broadway theaters in New York sold approximately 13.1 million tickets, generating $1.27 billion in gross revenue.

Now (2024): In the 2022-2023 season, Broadway theaters saw a total attendance of 12.3 million and generated $1.58 billion in gross revenue.

Tourism and GDP

Then (2014): Global tourism's direct contribution to GDP was around $2.4 trillion.

Now (2024): Despite a setback during the pandemic, in 2023 the travel and tourism industry's contribution to the global GDP is estimated to be 10.6%, or around $9.5 trillion.

Annual Passengers Carried by the Airline Industry

Then (2014): Airlines carried approximately 3.3 billion passengers.

Now (2024): The number of passengers has risen, with the airline industry expected to carry over 4 billion passengers annually.

Big Mac Index

Then (2014): In 2014, the average price of a Big Mac in the United States was around $4.80. In comparison, a Big Mac would have cost you $7.15—the second highest price in the world, due to high inflation at the time.

Now (2024): In 2024, the average price is $5.15, however, it varies between regions. Now, Venezuela has the world's cheapest Big Mac at $1.70.

Cruise Industry Passengers

Then (2014): The cruise industry carried about 22 million passengers.

Now (2024): In 2024, the cruise industry is anticipated to carry approximately 36 million passengers globally which is a 120% increase on pre-pandemic numbers.

Hotel Industry Revenue

Then (2014): The global hotel industry generated around $457 billion in revenue.

Now (2024): Despite a dip due to travel restrictions, the industry's revenue has seen a resurgence, with a greater emphasis on health and safety.

Commercial Long-haul Flights

Then (2014): In 2014, the longest commercial flight was the Qantas flight from Sydney to Dallas, which covered 8,575 miles (13,800 km) in around 16 hours, after Singapore Airlines discontinued its 18 hours and 25 minutes Singapore to Newark flight in 2013.

Now (2024): Singapore Airlines retook the crown in 2023 when it launched its 18 hour and 50 minute Singapore to New York JFK flight.

Average Global GDP Growth

Then (2014): The world GDP growth rate was 3.1%.

Now (2024): In 2024, the global GDP growth rate is forecasted to be 3.1%. This growth rate represents a slight improvement compared to 2023, but is still below the historical (2000-2019) average global GDP growth rate of 3.8%

Cost of 1GB Mobile Data

Then (2014): The global average cost for 1GB of mobile data was varied, with some countries averaging above $10.

Now (2024): With increased competition and technology improvements, the cost has decreased in many regions, with some countries offering data for less than $1 per GB. The United States remains one of the most expensive countries, with an average 1GB data cost of $5.62 in 2023.

Minimum Wage Comparisons

Then (2014): The federal minimum wage in the United States was $7.25 per hour. However, states and cities can specify their own minimum wages. California had a minimum wage of $8.00 per hour in 2014.

Now (2024): The federal minimum wage has remained the same since 2009. However, some states and cities have significantly increased their minimum wage, with movements advocating for higher living wages gaining traction. In 2024, the minimum wage in California is now $16 per hour—the largest increase of all the states.

Price of Gold per Ounce

Then (2014): The average price was approximately $1,266 per ounce.

Now (2024): Gold prices have fluctuated with economic conditions and global uncertainty, but reached $2,195.17per ounce in March 2024.

Average Monthly Rent for a One-Bedroom Apartment in New York City

Then (2014): In 2014, the average monthly rent for a one-bedroom apartment in Manhattan, New York City was around $3,100.

Now (2024): The average rent for a one-bedroom apartment in Manhattan reached a record high of $5,588 per month in 2023.

Oil Prices per Barrel

Then (2014): The price of Brent crude oil was below $50 per barrel.

Now (2024): Oil prices have seen dramatic volatility due to geopolitical events, production changes, and shifts towards renewable energy. As of March 29, 2024, the current price of crude oil is $83.17 per barrel, however, this is much lower than the price of $120 per barrel in mid-2022 due to the EU's sanctions on Russian oil.

Average Electric Costs — USA

Then (2014): The average cost of residential electricity in the US was 12.52 cents per Kilowatthour.

Now (2024): The average cost has increased to 15.98 cents per Kilowatthour, however, with the rise of energy-efficient appliances and solar panel installations, many households have seen lower electricity bills.

Cost of a Standard First-Class Stamp

Then (2014): In the United States, the cost was $0.49.

Now (2024): The price for postage has increased to $0.69.

Average New Car Price

Then (2014): The average sale price of a new car was approximately $32,000 in the United States.

Now (2024): With the advent of electric vehicles and advanced technology features, average prices have risen to $49,388.

Sources

Kemp, S. (2024). **Internet use in 2024 - DataReportal – Global Digital Insights.** https://datareportal.com/reports/digital-2024-deep-dive-the-state-of-internet-adoption

Renewables Now. (2014). **Renewables deliver 13.8% of global energy in 2014 - IEA.** https://renewablesnow.com/news/renewables-deliver-138-of-global-energy-in-2014-iea-534827/

Renewables in Electricity Production: Statistics Map by Region. (n.d.). https://yearbook.enerdata.net/renewables/renewable-in-electricity-production-share.html

Deguignet M., Juffe-Bignoli D., Harrison J., MacSharry B., Burgess N., Kingston N., (2014) **2014 United Nations List of Protected Areas. UNEP-WCMC: Cambridge, UK.**

Protected Planet. (2024). https://www.protectedplanet.net/en

Literacy rate, adult total (% of people ages 15 and above). (n.d.). https://data.worldbank.org/indicator/SE.ADT.LITR.ZS?view=chart

Clayton Wadsworth. (2022). **Visualizing 10 Years of Global EV Sales by Country. Retrieved from https://www.visualcapitalist.com/visualizing-10-years-of-global-ev-sales-by-country/**

Global EV Sales for 2023. (n.d.). https://www.ev-volumes.com/

NEW REPORT: IUCN's Tiger Programme finds there has been an average increase of the tiger population within project sites by 40% between 2015 and 2021. (2021). https://www.iucn.org/news/species/202107/new-report-iucns-tiger-programme-finds-there-has-been-average-increase-tiger-population-within-project-sites-40-between-2015-and-2021

Brigida, D. (2023). **New tiger population estimate of 5,574 wild tigers announced by Global Tiger Forum.** https://www.worldwildlife.org/stories/new-tiger-population-estimate-of-5-574-wild-tigers-announced-by-global-tiger-forum

Voyager - Mission Status. (n.d.).
https://voyager.jpl.nasa.gov/mission/status/
Dixon, S. J. (2024). **"Biggest social media platforms 2024."** https://www.statista.com/statistics/272014/global-social-networks-ranked-by-number-of-users/

Meta Investor Relations. (2014). https://investor.fb.com/investor-news/press-release-details/2015/Facebook-Reports-Fourth-Quarter-and-Full-Year-2014-Results/

Life Expectancy of the World Population. (n.d.). https://www.worldometers.info/demographics/life-expectancy/

World Population Facts. (2023). Retrieved from https://populationmatters.org/lp-the-facts/

X, S. (2024). **Deforestation in Brazilian Amazon halved in 2023.** https://phys.org/news/2024-01-deforestation-brazilian-amazon-halved.html

Artificial Intelligence Market Size & Trends, Growth Analysis, Forecast [2030]. (n.d.). https://www.marketsandmarkets.com/Market-Reports/artificial-intelligence-market-74851580.html

ThinkingView. (2017). **Global mobile statistics 2014 Part A: Mobile subscribers; handset market share; mobile operators.** https://mobiforge.com/research-analysis/global-mobile-statistics-2014-part-a-mobile-subscribers-handset-market-share-mobile-operators

Taylor, P. (2024). **Mobile phone subscriptions worldwide 2023.** Retrieved from https://www.statista.com/statistics/262950/global-mobile-subscriptions-since-1993/

Homicide Rate, 1950–2014. (n.d.). https://www.infoplease.com/us/crime/homicide-rate-1950-2014

US Murder Rates 2023. https://www.axios.com/2023/12/28/us-murder-violent-crime-rates-drop

Ritchie, H., & Roser, M. (2024). **Obesity.** https://ourworldindata.org/obesity

Koliaki, C., Dalamaga, M., & Liatis, S. (2023). **Current Obesity Reports, 12(4), 514–527. doi:10.1007/s13679-023-00527-y**

Armstrong, M., & Richter, F. (2023). **Infographic: Global Internet Speeds Rising Rapidly.** https://www.statista.com/chart/31075/global-average-internet-download-speed/
Hong, K. (2014). **Akamai: Global Average Web Speed Up 24% to 3.9 Mbps. Retrieved from https://thenextweb.com/news/akamai-global-average-internet-speed-24-year-year-3-9-mbps-mobile**

Space debris by the numbers. (n.d.). https://www.esa.int/Space_Safety/Space_Debris/Space_debris_by_the_numbers

Iea. (2023). **Trends in charging infrastructure – Global EV Outlook 2023 – Analysis.** https://www.iea.org/reports/global-ev-outlook-2023/trends-in-charging-infrastructure

Global Wind Report (2014). https://www.gwec.net/wp-content/uploads/2015/03/GWEC_Global_Wind_2014_Report_LR.pdf

Alexandrou, D. (2023). **1TW Celebration.** https://gwec.net/1twcelebration/

Forest area (% of land area). (n.d.). https://data.worldbank.org/indicator/AG.LND.FRST.ZS

Plastics in a Circular Economy (2014). https://www.europarl.europa.eu/RegData/etudes/BRIE/2017/603940/EPRS_BRI(2017)603940_EN.pdf

Environment, U. (n.d.). **Drowning in Plastics – Marine Litter and Plastic Waste Vital Graphics.** https://www.unep.org/resources/report/drowning-plastics-marine-litter-and-plastic-waste-vital-graphics

Best, R. de. (2024). **Crypto users worldwide 2016-2023.** https://www.statista.com/statistics/1202503/global-cryptocurrency-user-base/

Centre, U. W. H. (n.d.). World Heritage List Statistics. Retrieved from https://whc.unesco.org/en/list/stat

Iea. (2015). **Global energy-related emissions of carbon dioxide stalled in 2014 - News.** https://www.iea.org/news/global-energy-related-emissions-of-carbon-dioxide-stalled-in-2014

Iea. (2023). **Executive Summary – CO2 Emissions in 2023 – Analysis.** https://www.iea.org/reports/co2-emissions-in-2023/executive-summary

Global unemployment rate set to increase in 2024 while growing social inequalities raise concerns, says ILO report. (2024). https://www.ilo.org/global/about-the-ilo/newsroom/news/WCMS_908068/
Greenhalgh, E. (n.d.). **2014 State of the Climate: Sea Level.** https://www.climate.gov/news-features/understanding-climate/2014-state-climate-sea-level

Preston, J. Et al. (2023). **Innovation at Illumina: The road to the $600 human genome.** https://www.nature.com/articles/d42473-021-00030-9

Publishing, B. (2018). **Virtual and Augmented Reality: Technologies and Global Markets.** https://www.bccresearch.com/market-research/information-technology/virtual-and-augmented-reality-technologies-and-global-markets-report.html

Hadhazy, A. (2019). **Meet the Exoplanet Class of 2014.** https://www.discover-magazine.com/the-sciences/meet-the-exoplanet-class-of-2014

Discoveries - Exoplanet Exploration: Planets Beyond our Solar System. (2022). https://exoplanets.nasa.gov/exoplanet-discoveries/

World Health Organization. **World malaria report 2014.** (2014). https://www.who.int/publications/i/item/9789241564830

World Health Organization. **World malaria report 2023.** (2023). https://www.who.int/teams/global-malaria-programme/reports/world-malaria-report-2023

More, P. by mobiThinkingView. (2017). **Global mobile statistics 2014 Part A: Mobile subscribers; handset market share; mobile operators.** https://mobiforge.com/research-analysis/global-mobile-statistics-2014-part-a-mobile-subscribers-handset-market-share-mobile-operators

Laricchia, F. (2023). **Global smartphone penetration 2016-2022.** https://www.statista.com/statistics/203734/global-smartphone-penetration-per-capita-since-2005/

NCEI.Monitoring.Info. (n.d.). **Annual 2023 Global Climate Report.** https://www.ncei.noaa.gov/access/monitoring/monthly-report/global/202313

Duarte, F. (2023). **Amount of Data Created Daily** (2024). https://explodingtopics.com/blog/data-generated-per-day#how-much

Infographic: How much data is produced every day? (2024). https://cloudtweaks.com/2015/03/how-much-data-is-produced-every-day/

School enrollment, primary (% net). (n.d.). https://data.worldbank.org/indicator/SE.PRM.NENR

Press Release: Online Learning Survey Report 2014. https://onlinelearningconsortium.org/press-release-online-learning-survey-report-2014/

E-Learning Market Trends & Forecasts 2014-2016 Report. (n.d.). https://campus.paho.org/en/e-learning-market-trends-forecasts-2014-2016-report

Global Terrorism Index: Countries most impacted by terrorism. (2024). https://www.visionofhumanity.org/maps/global-terrorism-index/#/

Global Terrorism Index 2024 - World. Retrieved from https://reliefweb.int/report/world/global-terrorism-index-2024

ReportBuyer. (2018). **Mobile Health (mHealth) Market Forecast 2014-2024 : A Revolution in eHealth, Telemedicine, Informatics & Connected Health.** https://www.prnewswire.com/news-releases/mobile-health-mhealth-market-forecast-2014-2024--a-revolution-in-ehealth-telemedicine-informatics--connected-health-277833001.html

Sukhanova, K. (2024). **Telemedicine Statistics - The Latest Telehealth Statistics in 2024. https://techreport.com/statistics/telemedicine-statistics/**

The IUCN Red List of Threatened Species. (n.d.). https://www.iucnredlist.org/about/background-history

Buchholz, K., & Richter, F. (2023). **Infographic: Number of Threatened Species is Rising.** https://www.statista.com/chart/17122/number-of-threatened-species-red-list/

Mosby, A., (2023). **42+ E-commerce Growth Statistics 2024 (Key Data Revealed).** https://www.yaguara.co/e-commerce-growth-statistics/

Nick. (2018). **The Global cost of cybercrime jumped up to $600 Billion.** https://www.cyberdefensemagazine.com/the-global-cost-of-cybercrime-jumped-up-to-600-billion/

Fox, J. (2024). **Top Cybersecurity Statistics for 2024.** https://www.cobalt.io/blog/cybersecurity-statistics-2024

Wildwood, L. (2024). **21 Top Book Sales Statistics For 2024 (Latest Industry Data).** https://bloggingwizard.com/book-sales-statistics/

Spangler, T. (2015). **Netflix Tops 57 Million Subscribers in Q4 as U.S. Growth Slows.** https://variety.com/2015/digital/news/netflix-tops-57-million-subscribers-in-q4-as-u-s-growth-slows-1201409712/
Netflix Statistics 2024 (2024). https://www.independent.co.uk/advisor/vpn/netflix-statistics

Movie Market Summary 1995 to 2024. (n.d.). https://www.the-numbers.com/market/

McClintock, P. (2023). **Box Office: 2014 to End Down Sharply Despite Holiday Highs.** https://www.hollywoodreporter.com/movies/movie-news/box-office-2014-end-down-760445/

Movie Market Summary 1995 to 2024. (n.d.). https://www.the-numbers.com/market/

Smirke, R. (2024). **IFPI Global Report 2024: Music Revenues Climb 10% to $28.6 Billion.** https://www.billboard.com/business/business-news/ifpi-global-report-2024-music-business-revenue-market-share-1235637873/

Duarte, F. (2024). **Music Streaming Services Stats (2024).** https://explodingtopics.com/blog/music-streaming-stats

Götting, M. C. (2015). **Global music streaming revenue growth by type 2014.** https://www.statista.com/statistics/421020/global-music-streaming-revenue-by-type/

13 Podcast Statistics You Need To Know For 2024. (2024). https://backlinko.com/podcast-stats#podcast-growth

55+ Top Podcasts to Listen to in 2024 (According to Genre). (n.d.). https://riverside.fm/blog/top-podcasts

Newsroom. (2013). https://web.archive.org/web/20131031180402/http://www.gartner.com/newsroom/id/2614915

Spark, A. A. (2024). **Global Video Game Market on the Rise in 2024 with a 2.8% Growth Expected.** Retrieved from https://www.linkedin.com/pulse/global-video-game-market-rise-2024-28-growth-expected-adasaispark-minee/

The Audiobook Market, and Its Revenue, Keep Growing. (2023). https://www.publishersweekly.com/pw/by-topic/industry-news/audio-books/article/92444-the-audiobook-market-and-revenue-keeps-growing.html
Koblin, J. (2015). **How Many Scripted TV Shows in 2015? A Precise Number, and a Record.** https://www.nytimes.com/2015/12/17/business/media/how-many-scripted-tv-shows-in-2015-a-precise-number-and-a-record.html

The Broadway League. (2023). https://www.broadwayleague.com/research/grosses-broadway-nyc/

2022–2023 Broadway End-Of-Season Statistics Show That Broadway Had Attendance Of 12.3 Million And Grosses Of $1.58 Billion. (n.d.). https://www.broadwayleague.com/press/press-releases/20222023-broadway-end-of-season-statistics-show-that-broadway-had-attendance-of-123-million-and-grosses-of-158-billion/

World Travel & Tourism Council. (2024). News Article: World Travel & Tourism Council (WTTC). https://wttc.org/news-article/global-travel-and-tourism-catapults-into-2023-says-wttc

Yam Chhetri (2024). **Global Tourism Statistics 2024:Facts and Forecasts.** https://wptravel.io/global-tourism-industry-statistics/

Global Outlook for Air Transport (2023). https://www.iata.org/en/iata-repository/publications/economic-reports/global-outlook-for-air-transport---june-2023/

The World of Air Transport in 2014 (2014). https://www.icao.int/annual-report-2014/Pages/the-world-of-air-transport-in-2014.aspx

EIA.gov (2024). https://www.eia.gov/electricity/monthly/epm_table_grapher.php?t=epmt_5_3

Lindner, J. (2024). **Statistics About The Average Electric Bill Per Month • Gitnux.** https://gitnux.org/average-electric-bill-per-month/

Financial Samurai (2024). **The Average New Car Price Is Unbelievably High.** https://www.financialsamurai.com/average-new-car-price/

Book, K. B. (2018). **New-Car Transaction Prices up Nearly 1.5 Percent in March 2014, According to Kelley Blue Book.** https://www.prnewswire.com/news-releases/new-car-transaction-prices-up-nearly-15-percent-in-march-2014-according-to-kelley-blue-book-253328141.html

Science & Technology

As we race through the 2020s, the pace of innovation only accelerates, fueled by extraordinary leaps in science and technology.

Just think, only a couple of years ago, the idea of quantum computing was a distant dream, yet today, it's forging new frontiers in computing power.

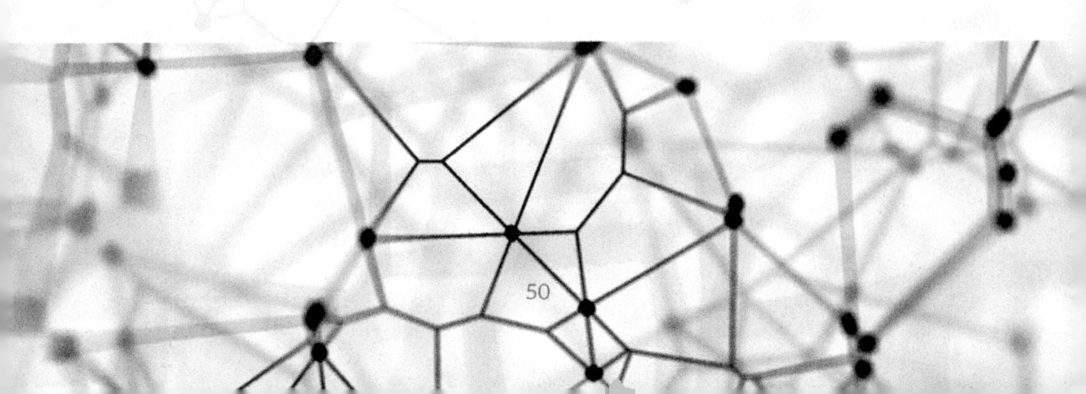

And who could have imagined that the integration of AI in everyday life, from bespoke shopping experiences to tailored medical treatments, would become so seamless?

The marvels of CRISPR gene editing have leapt from research papers to real-world applications, promising a revolution in healthcare. With immersive virtual reality experiences that are now indistinguishable from the real world, it's a time when science fiction becomes science fact.

Dive into these fascinating science and technology facts, and let's toast to the ingenuity that propels us into tomorrow.

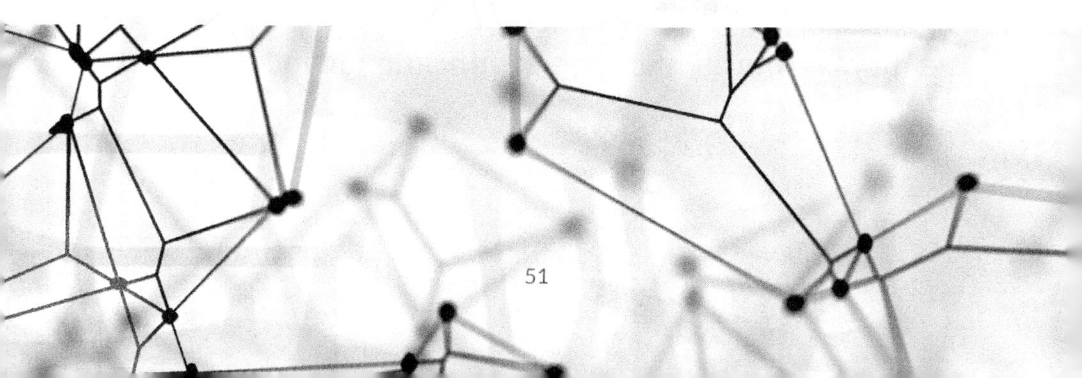

2023 was definitely the year of AI. The rapid development and widespread adoption of AI platforms like ChatGPT have infiltrated many scientific and technological domains. In fact, ChatGPT was shown to outperform human doctors when responding to online medical questions using quality and empathy as measures.

•••

In 2023, researchers from Cambridge mapped the entire neural network of an insect brain, providing unprecedented insight into neurological connectivity.

•••

In a pioneering 2023 study, University of Cambridge and Caltech teams engineered synthetic human embryos from stem cells, a significant advancement for medical research.

Two biological dads? It could be possible! 2023 saw geneticists at Osaka University achieving a first: creating viable mice offspring from two male parents, expanding the possibilities of reproductive science.

• • •

A team at the University of Minnesota successfully transplanted a cryogenically preserved rat kidney in 2023, marking a potential revolution in organ transplantation.

• • •

A worrying climatological record was set in 2023 when Antarctic sea ice shrank to its lowest-ever observed extent, prompting concerns about accelerating climate change.

In 2023, a paralysed man was able to walk again using only his thoughts, thanks to groundbreaking neural technology. Using brain and spinal implants, the man who had been paralysed for 10 years after an injury could walk again.

• • •

AI made a profound impact on cancer prevention in 2023, with the development of an algorithm that can predict pancreatic cancer risk years before a clinical diagnosis using patient medical records.

• • •

Progress in protein structure prediction made leaps in 2023, with AI reducing the list of unknown human protein structures from thousands to less than thirty, opening new doors in biological science.

The rollout and adoption of 5G networks continue to accelerate, with forecasts of 4.4 billion 5G subscriptions by 2027.

• • •

In 2023, the FDA approved the first nonprescription birth control pill and a rapid-acting medication for postpartum depression. The anti-depressant Zurzuvae can take effect in just three days rather than the two-plus weeks required for older medications.

• • •

Spaceflight turned a shade greener in 2023 with the successful launch of the methane-fueled Zhuque-2 rocket, signalling a shift towards more sustainable space exploration. Although methane is a greenhouse gas, it is considered to be much more environmentally friendly than the standard kerosene fuel used for most spaceflights.

India's space ambitions soared in 2023, with a landmark lunar landing near the moon's elusive south pole, a first in the history of space exploration. Previous attempts by India and Russia had both ended in crashes.

• • •

Commercial space travel reached new heights in 2023, as Virgin Galactic's spaceplane carried its first tourists, igniting the industry for space tourism. Hundreds of people are already on the waiting list for future flights, with tickets costing around $450,000.

• • •

In 2023, engineers unveiled a super bright white paint formulation capable of extreme reflectivity, which could potentially help keep cities cooler.

Alexander Graham Bell invented the metal detector in 1881 to help find a bullet that was lodged inside President James A. Garfield.

• • •

Scientists have recently discovered that a chain reaction of supernovae that occurred around 14 million years ago created a 1,000-light-year-wide bubble at the center of which lies our galaxy. All the local star-forming regions sit on its surface, providing the first explanation for the formation of stars in the Milky Way.

• • •

The famous Facebook 'like' button was almost called the 'awesome' button before Mark Zuckerberg vetoed it.

The food with the highest caloric value is pure animal fat, with nearly 900 calories per 100 grams.

• • •

When NASA's Perseverance rover arrived on Mars in 2020, it deployed a colourful parachute containing a coded message written in binary meaning 'dare mighty things'. It was taken from a quote by President Theodore Roosevelt.

• • •

Humans could never land on Jupiter, Saturn, Uranus or Neptune because they are made of gas and have no solid surface.

• • •

The smallest thing ever photographed was the shadow of an atom.

Adults spend nearly 50 per cent of their time letting their minds wander, according to a study from Harvard University, which tracked users via an app.

Every person is only 0.1 per cent genetically different from each other; our closest living relatives — chimpanzees — are 1.2 per cent different from us.

• • •

Approximately one per cent of descendants of Northern Europeans are immune to HIV. Swedes are the least likely to be infected.

• • •

If you could get into your car and drive 60 mph (96.5 km/h) straight up, it would only take one hour to reach outer space.

The average person checks their phone every six minutes.

• • •

The more full your fridge is, the more energy-efficient it is. This is because less air can escape.

• • •

There are towering mountains of ice on Pluto, such as those in the Sputnik Planitia region, which are composed of water ice and rise several kilometers high.

• • •

In Sweden, blood donors get a text message when their blood has been used in a patient.

Before the Pfizer coronavirus vaccine, which was developed and licensed within 11 months in December 2020, the fastest vaccine to go to market was for mumps, taking four years in 1967.

• • •

Astrophysical discoveries in 2023 included the detection of methyl cation in a young star system by the James Webb Space Telescope, enhancing our understanding of molecular formation in space.

• • •

In a milestone for geology, scientists drilled into Earth's mantle for the first time in 2023, gaining invaluable direct samples from beneath the ocean floor.

In 2023, Chinese scientists were able to grow part-human kidneys within pig embryos. The new kidneys were composed of up to 65 per cent human cells.

• • •

GPS may be free to use, but it costs around $2 million per day to run. GPS is a constellation of 24 satellites, which initially cost $12 billion to put into orbit.

• • •

The only letter that is not in the periodic table is J.

• • •

The first letter to be sent over the internet was 'L'.

• • •

Water is repelled by a magnet. Try it.

A study found that if you look at a photo of a loved one, you can reduce pain by around 40 per cent.
If you could throw a snowball fast enough it would completely vaporise when it hit a brick wall.

• • •

Just over two-thirds of cancer patients treated in the USA are cured.

• • •

The sky on Mars is red and the sunsets are blue. This is due to the type of dust in the air there.

• • •

Up until the 1950s, many doctors believed exercise was dangerous for people over the age of 40. They would prescribe bed rest to heart disease sufferers.

Katy Sullivan, the first woman to walk in space, also became the first female to travel to Challenger Deep — the lowest reachable depth on Earth. While there, she had a call with the International Space Station.

• • •

Nomophobia is an addiction to mobile phones. Over 200,000 people suffer from this phobia, which leaves you afraid to leave your home without your mobile phone.

• • •

92 per cent of the world's currency exists digitally — the rest is physical money.

• • •

Venus is the only planet in the solar system that spins backwards.

A Japanese Google employee, Emma Haruka Iwao, calculated Pi to a record 31 trillion digits using the company's cloud computing service.

• • •

US astronauts at the International Space Station are sent ballot papers to allow them to vote in elections.

• • •

If you spin a ball as you drop it, it will fly. This is called the Magnus effect.

• • •

Water can boil and freeze at the same time when at certain pressures.

There are more mobile phone connections than people in the world.

• • •

In our galaxy alone there are over 100 billion planets.

• • •

Over three billion people in the world use a mobile phone. Three and a half billion use a toothbrush.

• • •

Popping a cork from a champagne bottle releases the same level of shock waves as a jet.

• • •

In the UK, over 86 per cent of breast cancer patients now survive for at least five years.

Scientists were able to reverse-engineer chickens to have dinosaur snouts.

• • •

Some flowers smell like chocolate, including the Chocolate Daisy and the Chocolate Cosmos.

• • •

An owl can hear a mouse more than 50 feet away.

• • •

If you crack an egg underwater, it looks like a jellyfish.

• • •

People who can function on only a few hours of sleep a night may have a gene mutation, according to a 2019 study.

Lasers can get trapped in a waterfall — an example of total internal reflection.

• • •

Certain types of beer have the same microbial and probiotic benefits as food products such as sauerkraut, yoghurt and kimchi.

• • •

Before 1995, domain name registrations were free!

• • •

A new beetle discovered by scientists in 2019 was named after Greta Thunberg. The Nelloptodes gretae has antennae that look like braided hair — the most popular style worn by the young activist.

Sodium in cheese can protect your body from cardiovascular disease caused by other salts.

• • •

If you squeeze lemon juice on apples and bananas you can prevent them from turning brown (oxidation).

• • •

The longest ever spacewalk lasted around nine hours.

• • •

A small percentage of the static you see on 'dead' TV stations is leftover radiation from the Big Bang.

Email existed before the World Wide Web.

• • •

There are 20 to 30 times more bacteria on the average mobile phone than what you find in a toilet bowl.

• • •

QWERTY keyboards were invented partially to slow down how fast you could type. This was because people were typing too fast and jamming their typewriters.

• • •

The first-ever personal computer was called 'Simon'.

If you use a lighter style font when printing, you can save up to 10 per cent ink so your printer cartridges will last longer.

• • •

In 1956, 5MB of data literally weighed a tonne and required a forklift to move it.

• • •

Over 90 per cent of text messages sent are read within three minutes of being delivered, and 99 per cent are ever read.

• • •

Mars is covered in rust, which is why it appears red.

Osmium and iridium are the densest metals in the world, while plutonium and uranium are the heaviest metals based on relative atomic mass.

• • •

One in three deaths around the world is caused by cardiovascular disease.

• • •

The dots in Gmail addresses are redundant. For example, if your email address is joebloggs@gmail.com, someone could email joe.bloggs.@gmail.com and it would still get to you.

• • •

Human bodies can move for more than a year after death. Don't be alarmed though, this is caused by the body's ligaments shrinking, drying out and contracting.

700 million years ago, Venus may have been hospitable.

• • •

When you move your eyes, your eardrums also move.

• • •

A 'jiffy' is an actual unit of time. It has been redefined over the years but was originally defined as the time it takes for light to travel one centimetre in a vacuum.

• • •

Some studies have shown that intelligent people have more copper and zinc in their hair.

Time slows down near black holes. Inside of them, it completely stops.

• • •

When lightning strikes a sandy beach that is high in silica or quartz, it produces glass.

• • •

A hurricane can produce as much energy as 10,000 nuclear bombs during its life cycle.

• • •

On average, humans remember 5,000 different faces.

• • •

It's impossible to burp in space.

Komodo dragons have a suit of armour made of tiny bones underneath their already scaly skin.

•••

In zero gravity conditions, a candle's flame is blue and round, because fire behaves differently in space.

•••

More lifeforms are living on your skin than people on the planet. Most of the time we have over 90 trillion microbes living on us.

•••

Goats can snack on poison ivy with no issues.

The US has blown up multiple atomic and hydrogen bombs in space. The most famous was in 1962, 250 miles above the Pacific Ocean. There is some spectacular video footage if you search online.

• • •

Strawberries are the only fruits that have their seeds on the outside.

• • •

Two million blood cells die every second. It's ok though—two million blood cells are also created every second.

• • •

It takes about 168 litres (37 gallons) of water to produce a single cup of coffee.

You can clean your toilet using Gatorade. Simply pour two cups of the drink into the toilet and leave for one hour, then brush away.

• • •

Hot water freezes faster than cold water. This is called the Mbemba effect.

• • •

The Dvorak keyboard is 74% faster to type on than the QWERTY keyboard, once you have completed training.

• • •

There are more nerve connectors in your brain than there are stars in the galaxy. A piece of brain tissue the size of a grain of sand contains over 100,000 neurons.

Diamonds can grow inside other diamonds. The first example was found in 2019.

• • •

Shaking your head after getting water in your ears may cause brain damage.

• • •

If you put grapes in the microwave they will explode.

• • •

An ear of corn always has an even number of rows (usually from 8 to 22) and an average of 800 kernels.

• • •

Everyone has a unique tongue print, just like a fingerprint.

If you removed all the empty space inside of humans, the entire human race would fit into the volume of a sugar cube. This is because we are 99.9999999999% empty matter.

• • •

There is a disease called Alien Hand Syndrome (AHS), in which the person has no conscious control over his 'alien hand' and will blurt things out like: "I swear I'm not doing this". It is also known as Dr Strangelove Syndrome.

• • •

The Bee Gees' song Stayin' Alive is used to train medical professionals to provide the correct number of chest compressions per minute while performing CPR.

Just 100 nanograms of botulinum toxin — the most deadly toxin in the world — could kill a human being. Just 1kg could wipe out the entire human race. However, people willfully use it in the form of Botox to freeze muscles in their faces to reduce wrinkles.

• • •

Every hour, there are around 760 thunderstorms on Earth.

• • •

The hardest working muscles in the human body are in the eyes. In one hour of reading, the eye makes nearly 10,000 movements.

• • •

There are more drops of water in the ocean than there are atoms in a drop of water, but only just!

California supplies over 80 per cent of the USA's broccoli.

• • •

Measured by weight, there will be more plastic in the oceans than there are fish by 2050.

• • •

If you take part in physical exercise four hours after learning something, it has been shown to help improve your long-term memory.

• • •

Feet have the highest concentration of sweat glands of any part of the body and can produce more than a pint of sweat a day.

When you see most stars, you're essentially looking hundreds or thousands of years into the past, as that's how long the light takes to reach us.

• • •

Rabies has a fatality rate of almost 100%.

• • •

It takes 17 muscles to smile and 43 to frown. So, smile more!

• • •

If you cut up a hologram, the entire image is retained in each piece.

The Pratfall Effect is a psychological phenomenon whereby a person who is deemed attractive or competent by someone is found to be even more so if they commit a blunder, such as tripping over.

•••

People don't get sick from cold weather; they get sick because viruses thrive better in cooler air. Also, we spend more time indoors when it's cold, and are in closer contact with infected people.

•••

Females are generally better at recognising different tastes than males.

•••

A study found that hard-to-read handwriting is more convincing, as the reader has to read slower and consider the argument more carefully.

Some spiders can make milk for their babies.

• • •

Men who look up to superheroes often have a more positive body image.

• • •

In June 2022, scientists published a study revealing the discovery of giant bacteria that can be seen without a microscope, challenging the belief that all bacteria are too small to be seen by the naked eye. The species thiomargarita magnifica grows to an average length of 0.35 inches (0.9 cm). The bacteria was first discovered in a Caribbean mangrove forest in 2009, but it took scientists time to realize that it was a bacteria due to its large size.

A set of human lungs has a surface area around 180 m^2, similar to that of a tennis court.

• • •

The largest snowflake ever recorded measured 15 inches (35 cm) across. It was discovered by a ranch owner in Montana in 1887.

• • •

The average human body contains enough fat to make seven bars of soap.

• • •

Dirty snow melts faster than clean snow because the dark colour absorbs more energy from the sun.

In May 2022, scientists took a picture of a black hole in the center of the Milky Way galaxy for the first time.

• • •

Since being discovered in 1930, Pluto has not yet completed a full orbit of the Sun. One Plutonian year is 247.68 Earth years.

• • •

Babies start dreaming before they are born.

• • •

Scientists at Columbia University have been able to grow heart muscle from human stem cells.

• • •

Men are more likely to develop long-term hiccups than women.

In 2022, a clinical trial discovered a partially effective treatment for Alzheimer's disease, where an antibody-drug reduced cognitive decline by 27% in 1,800 early-stage Alzheimer's patients over 18 months. However, the treatment also has risks, including brain bleeds and swelling, and 7% of patients had to stop the treatment due to side effects.

• • •

When glass breaks, the cracks move at speeds of up to 3,000 miles per hour (4,828 km/h).

• • •

In one acre (0.4 hectares) of land, there can be more than one million earthworms.

A study published in 2022 showed that half of the people tested had a type of plastic used in water bottles and food packaging in their blood.

• • •

When baby sharks are born, they swim away from their mothers and live on their own immediately.

• • •

It can take a photon (a light-carrying particle) 40,000 years to travel from the core of the sun to the surface, but only eight minutes to travel the rest of the way to earth.

• • •

In 1936, Russia built an analogue computer that ran on water called the Water Integrator. It could solve partial differential equations.

Honey contains hydrogen peroxide, which makes it a great natural antiseptic.

• • •

It is impossible to kill yourself by holding your breath.

• • •

The first computer programmers were women. Ada Lovelace was the first person to publish an algorithm to be executed by the world's first modern computer.

• • •

In 2022, US renewable sources such as hydropower, wind, and solar produced more power than coal and nuclear, making up more than a fifth of all electricity.

Peanuts are legumes and are not tree nuts.

• • •

Germany started using the first-ever hydrogen trains in 2022. These trains, which have 14 engines, replaced diesel trains on a train line close to Hamburg. They use fuel cells that mix hydrogen and oxygen to make electricity and only make water vapor as pollution.

• • •

There is around $771 trillion worth of gold floating in the oceans — but it's in such small pieces that it would be almost impossible to harvest.

The longest time that has gone between two twins being born was 87 days. They were born in Ireland in 2012.

• • •

There's enough water pressure in one onion cell to cause a steam engine to explode.

• • •

In 2022, NASA successfully hit an asteroid with a spacecraft in a test to protect Earth.

• • •

The human brain is capable of creating more connections than there are stars in the Milky Way galaxy.

Sources

Top 23 Scientific And Tech Developments Of 2023". 2023. *Interestingengineering.Com.* https://interestingengineering.com/lists/top-23-scientific-tech-2023.

Winding, M., Pedigo, B. D., Barnes, C. L., Patsolic, H. G., Park, Y., Kazimiers, T., ... & Zlatic, M. (2023). *Science, 379(6636).* https://doi.org/10.1126/science.add9330.

"10 Scientific Discoveries In 2023". 2023. *Laboratoryequipment.Com.* https://www.laboratoryequipment.com/608790-10-Scientific-Discoveries-in-2023/.

Duggal, N. (2024). "22 New Technology Trends For 2024: New Tech Horizons". *Simplilearn.Com.* https://www.simplilearn.com/top-technology-trends-and-jobs-article.

Ledford, H., & Kozlov, M. (2023). "The Mice With Two Dads: Scientists Create Eggs From Male Cells". *Nature.Com.* https://www.nature.com/articles/d41586-023-00717-7.

"Long-Last Ocean Drillers Exhume Bounty Of Rocks From Earth's Mantle". 2023. *Science.Org.* https://www.science.org/content/article/long-last-ocean-drillers-exhume-bounty-rocks-earth-s-mantle.

Whang, O. (2023). "Brain Implants Allow Paralyzed Man To Walk Using His Thoughts". *Nytimes.com.* https://www.nytimes.com/2023/05/24/science/paralysis-brain-implants-ai.html.

Belluck, P. (2023). "For The First Time, There's A Pill For Postpartum Depression". *Nytimes.com.* https://www.nytimes.com/2023/08/04/health/postpartum-depression-pill-fda.html.

Jones, A. (2023). "China's Landspace Reaches Orbit With Methane-Powered Zhuque-2 Rocket". *Spacenews.com.* https://spacenews.com/chinas-landspace-reaches-orbit-with-methane-powered-zhuque-2-rocket/.

Kumar, H., Travelli, A., Mashal, M., & Chang, K. (2023). "India Is On The Moon": Lander's Success Moves Nation To Next Space Chapter". *Nytimes.com.* https://www.nytimes.com/2023/08/23/science/chandrayaan-3-india-moon-landing.html.

"Virgin Galactic Completes First Private Astronaut Spaceflight Galactic-02". N.d. *Virgingalactic.Com.* https://www.virgingalactic.com/news/virgin-galactic-completes-first-private-astronaut-spaceflight-galactic-02.

Buckley, C. (2023). "To Help Cool A Hot Planet, The Whitest Of White Coats". Nytimes.Com. https://www.nytimes.com/2023/07/12/climate/white-paint-climate-cooling.html.

Kalisher, R., Cradic, M. S., Adams, M. J., Martin, M. A., & Finkelstein, I. (2023). "One Of The World's Earliest Cases Of Brain Surgery". *Plos One, 18(2).* https://doi.org/10.1371/journal.pone.0281020.

Rossen, J. (2023). "Scientific Progress Goes "Oink": Part-Human Kidneys Have Been Grown In Pig Embryos". *Mentalfloss.com.* https://www.mentalfloss.com/posts/pigs-grow-human-kidneys.

"22 Things That Happened For The First Time In 2022". 2022. Nytimes. Com. https://www.nytimes.com/2022/12/06/special-series/2022-firsts-year-in-review.html. "James A. Garfield". 2022. *Clintonwhitehouse3.Archives.Gov.* https://clintonwhitehouse3.archives.gov/WH/glimpse/presidents/html/jg20.html.

"Facts And Figures 2021". 2022. *Itu.Int.* https://www.itu.int/itu-d/reports/statistics/facts-figures-2021/.

"There's A Lost Continent Hiding Beneath Europe". 2019. *Livescience.Com.* https://www.livescience.com/ancient-lost-continent-beneath-europe.html.

"Calories In 100 G Of Animal Fat Or Drippings And Nutrition Facts". 2022. *Fatsecret.Com.* https://www.fatsecret.com/calories-nutrition/generic/animal-fat-or-drippings?portionid=55830&portionamount=100.000.

"First photo of shadow of single atom". 2022. *Sciencedaily.com.* https://www.sciencedaily.com/releases/2012/07/120703172543.htm

"Billions And Billions Of Planets". 2022. *NASA.* https://www.nasa.gov/mission_pages/kepler/news/kepler20130103.html#.UrIUHmRDtWZ.

"Far From Special: Humanity's Tiny DNA Differences Are 'Average' In Animal Kingdom". 2022. *Phys.Org.* https://phys.org/news/2018-05-special-humanity-tiny-dna-differences.html.

Nast, Condé. 2005. **"Genetic HIV Resistance Deciphered"**. *Wired.* https://www.wired.com/2005/01/genetic-hiv-resistance-deciphered/.

"Billions And Billions Of Planets". 2022. *NASA*. https://www.nasa.gov/mission_pages/kepler/news/kepler20130103.html#.UrIUHmRDtWZ.

"Now Blood Donors Can Get A Text When They Save Lives". 2022. *Time*. https://time.com/3943272/blood-donation-sweden-text/.

"What Would Happen If Humans Tried To Land On Jupiter". 2022. *Business Insider*. https://www.businessinsider.com/what-would-happen-if-humans-tried-landing-on-jupiter-space-2018-2

Fisher, Len. 2022. **"How Long Does It Take To Get To The Moon If You Drive At 60Mph?"**. *BBC Science Focus Magazine*. https://www.sciencefocus.com/space/if-you-could-drive-a-car-upwards-at-60mph-how-long-would-it-take-to-get-to-the-moon/.
Aislinn Antrim, Assistant Editor. 2020. "**Study: More Wine, Cheese In Diet Can Reduce Cognitive Decline"**. *Pharmacy Times*. https://www.pharmacytimes.com/view/study-including-more-wine-cheese-in-diet-can-reduce-cognitive-decline.

Garber, Megan. 2014. "**The First Characters Sent Through The Internet Were L-O-L"**. *The Atlantic*. https://www.theatlantic.com/technology/archive/2014/10/the-first-characters-sent-through-the-internet-were-l-o-l/382074/.

"How Many Faces Do People Know? | Proceedings Of The Royal Society B: Biological Sciences". 2022. *Proceedings Of The Royal Society B*. https://royalsocietypublishing.org/doi/full/10.1098/rspb.2018.1319.

"Mars Decoder Ring – NASA'S Mars Exploration Program". 2022. *NASA'S Mars Exploration Program*. https://mars.nasa.gov/resources/25646/mars-decoder-ring/.

"Don't Take Your Head Out Of The Clouds!". 2021. *Nytimes.Com*. https://www.nytimes.com/2021/04/10/at-home/daydreaming.html.

Magazine, Smithsonian, and Jason Daley. 2019. **"Venus Could Have Been Habitable For Billions Of Years"**. *Smithsonian Magazine*. https://www.smithsonianmag.com/smart-news/venus-could-have-been-habitable-billions-years-180973203/.

Gruters, Kurtis G., David L. K. Murphy, Cole D. Jenson, David W. Smith, Christopher A. Shera, and Jennifer M. Groh. 2018. **"The Eardrums Move When The Eyes Move: A Multisensory Effect On The Mechanics Of Hearing"**. *Proceedings Of The National Academy Of Sciences 115* (6): E1309-E1318. doi:10.1073/pnas.1717948115.

"Americans Check Their Phones 96 Times A Day". 2022. *Prnewswire.Com*. https://www.prnewswire.com/news-releases/americans-check-their-phones-96-times-a-day-300962643.html.

"Techcrunch Is Part Of The Yahoo Family Of Brands". 2022. *Techcrunch. Com*. https://techcrunch.com/2010/10/05/awesome-this-post/.

"How Much Does GPS Cost? | TIME.Com". 2022. *TIME.Com*. https://nation.time.com/2012/05/21/how-much-does-gps-cost/.

CY, Chang, Ke DS, and Chen JY. 2009. **"Essential Fatty Acids And Human Brain"**. *Acta Neurologica Taiwanica 18 (4)*. https://pubmed.ncbi.nlm.nih.gov/20329590/

"Potential Energy Source For Life Spotted On Saturn Moon Enceladus". 2017. *Space*.Com. https://www.space.com/36455-saturn-moon-enceladus-energy-source-life.html.

You, Jia. 2022. **"2017 In Science: Breakthroughs, Breakdowns, And More"**. *Vis.Sciencemag.Org*. https://vis.sciencemag.org/breakthrough2017/finalists/#cosmic-convergence.
"Do Magnets Work Under Water?". 2022. *Terpconnect.Umd.Edu*. https://terpconnect.umd.edu/~wbreslyn/magnets/do-magnets-work-under-water.html.

"Love can relieve pain". 2022. *The New York Times*. https://well.blogs.nytimes.com/2010/10/13/love-and-pain-relief/.

"5 Tips to Make Your Refrigerator More Efficient". 2022. *Thekitchn.com*. https://www.thekitchn.com/5-tips-on-organizing-your-frid-154587.

"20 Out Of Last 22 Years Warmest On Record". *Deccan Herald*. https://www.deccanherald.com/national/20-out-last-22-years-warmest-706147.html.

Pardo, Dimas. 2018. **"12 Mobile Phone Facts That Will Shock You, Keep Reading To Find Out"**. *Ehorus*. https://ehorus.com/mobile-phone-facts/.

"Cancer Treatment At The End Of Life (Published 2019)". 2019. *Nytimes. Com*. https://www.nytimes.com/2019/08/05/well/live/cancer-treatment-at-the-end-of-life.html.

"How Many Steps Should You Take A Day? (Published 2019)". 2019. *Nytimes.Com*. https://www.nytimes.com/2019/08/21/magazine/how-many-steps-should-you-take-a-day.html.

Hernandez, Ivan, and Jesse Lee Preston. 2013. **"Disfluency Disrupts The Confirmation Bias"**. *Journal Of Experimental Social Psychology 49 (1)*: 178-182. doi:10.1016/j.jesp.2012.08.010.

"Prolonged Milk Provisioning In A Jumping Spider". 2022. *Science*. https://www.science.org/doi/10.1126/science.aat3692.

Young, Ariana F., Shira Gabriel, and Jordan L. Hollar. 2013. **"Batman To The Rescue! The Protective Effects Of Parasocial Relationships With Muscular Superheroes On Men's Body Image"**. *Journal Of Experimental Social Psychology 49 (1)*: 173-177. doi:10.1016/j.jesp.2012.08.003.

"5 Amazing Things We'Ve Learned A Year After Visiting Pluto". 2022. *Science*. https://www.nationalgeographic.com/science/article/pluto-planets-new-horizons-one-year-anniversary-nasa-space-science.

"92% Of The World's Currency Is Digital - 12 Weird But True Facts About Technology | The Times Of India". 2022. *The Times Of India*. https://timesofindia.indiatimes.com/12-weird-but-true-facts-about-technology/92-of-the-worlds-currency-is-digital/photostory/51422304.cms.

Franzen, Harald. 2001. **"Why Venus Spins The Wrong Way"**. *Scientific American*. https://www.scientificamerican.com/article/why-venus-spins-the-wrong/.
"Emma Haruka Iwao Smashes Pi World Record With Google Help". 2022. *BBC News*. https://www.bbc.com/news/technology-47524760.

Voytko, Lisette. 2022. **"Astronaut Casts Election Day Vote From International Space Station"**. *Forbes*. https://www.forbes.com/sites/lisettevoytko/2019/11/05/astronaut-casts-election-day-vote-from-international-space-station/?sh=6971d2d815d6.

"Magnus Effect | Definition, Examples, & Facts". 2022. *Encyclopedia Britannica*. https://www.britannica.com/science/Magnus-effect.

"'Human-Sized Penguin' Lived In New Zealand". 2022. *BBC News*. https://www.bbc.com/news/world-asia-49340715.

"How Many People Have Smartphones Worldwide (Feb 2022)". 2022. *Bankmycell.Com*. https://www.bankmycell.com/blog/how-many-phones-are-in-the-world.

"Breast Cancer Survival Statistics". 2015. *Cancer Research UK*. https://www.cancerresearchuk.org/health-professional/cancer-statistics/statistics-by-cancer-type/breast-cancer/survival#heading-Zero.

"Best Chocolate Scented Flowers To Make A Chocolate Garden". 2019. *Balcony Garden Web*. https://balconygardenweb.com/best-chocolate-scented-flowers-plants-and-flowers-that-smell-like-flower/.

"Under-Expanded Supersonic CO2 Freezing Jets During Champagne Cork Popping". 2022. *Science Advances*. https://www.science.org/doi/10.1126/sciadv.aav5528.

"Will Space Be Kept Clean Of Debris? Americans Are Skeptical". 2018. *Pew Research Center*. https://www.pewresearch.org/fact-tank/2018/08/31/as-debris-piles-up-americans-are-skeptical-enough-will-be-done-to-limit-space-junk/.

2022. *Youtube.Com*. https://www.youtube.com/watch?v=rJmoROaMduQ.

"A Brief History Of The Domain Name". 2014. *Mashable*. https://mashable.com/archive/domain-names-history.

"Lemon Juice On Apples Experiment | HST Learning Center". 2017. *Home Science Tools Homeschool Hub*. https://learning-center.homesciencetools.com/article/acid-keeps-apple-fresh/.

"20 Fascinating Facts That Will Make You Think Twice". 2015. *The Independent*. https://www.independent.co.uk/news/weird-news/20-fascinating-facts-that-will-make-you-think-twice-a6747011.html.

Shi, Guangsen, Lijuan Xing, David Wu, Bula J. Bhattacharyya, Christopher R. Jones, Thomas McMahon, and S.Y. Christin Chong et al. 2019. **"A Rare Mutation Of B1-Adrenergic Receptor Affects Sleep/Wake Behaviors"**. *Neuron* 103 (6): 1044-1055.e7. doi:10.1016/j.neuron.2019.07.026.

"Scientists Say If You Drink This Beer Every Day It Would Be 'Very Good For You'". 2019. *The Independent*. https://www.independent.co.uk/life-style/food-and-drink/beer-healthy-probiotic-belgian-beers-hoegaarden-westmalle-eric-claasen-gut-a9227106.html.

"Michael Darby | Natural History Museum, London - Academia.Edu". 2022. *Nhm.Academia.Edu*. https://nhm.academia.edu/MichaelDarby.
Alba, Billie K, Anna E Stanhewicz, Priyankar Dey, Richard S Bruno, W Larry Kenney, and Lacy M Alexander. 2019.

"Controlled Feeding Of An 8-D, High-Dairy Cheese Diet Prevents Sodium-Induced Endothelial Dysfunction In The Cutaneous Microcirculation Of Healthy, Older Adults Through Reductions In Superoxide". *The Journal Of Nutrition* 150 (1): 55-63. doi:10.1093/jn/nxz205.

“Cast-Iron Cookware - Wikipedia”. 2021. *En.Wikipedia.Org*. https://en.wikipedia.org/wiki/Cast-iron_cookware.

“History of the Internet.” 2022. *Nethistory.Info*. http://www.nethistory.info/History%20of%20the%20Internet/email.html.

“12 Weird But True Facts About Technology - The Economic Times”. 2022. *The Economic Times*. https://economictimes.indiatimes.com/tech-life/12-weird-but-true-facts-about-technology/email-existed-before-the-world-wide-web/slideshow/51419395.cms.

“Edmund Berkeley Designs & Builds Simon, The First Personal Computer : History Of Information”. 1950. *Historyofinformation.Com*. https://www.historyofinformation.com/detail.php?entryid=95.

“Spam Statistics: Spam E-Mail Traffic Share 2021 | Statista”. 2022. *Statista*. https://www.statista.com/statistics/420391/spam-email-traffic-share/.

“10 Tips To Save On Ink When Printing | HP® Tech Takes”. 2022. *Hp.Com*. https://www.hp.com/us-en/shop/tech-takes/10-tips-save-on-ink-when-printing.

“What A 5MB Hard Drive Looked Like In 1956”. 2011. *TNW | Shareables*. https://thenextweb.com/news/this-is-what-a-5mb-hard-drive-looked-like-is-1956-required-a-forklift.

“What A 5MB Hard Drive Looked Like In 1956”. 2011. *TNW | Shareables*. https://thenextweb.com/news/this-is-what-a-5mb-hard-drive-looked-like-is-1956-required-a-forklift.
“Conversational Advertising.” 2022. *Mobilesquared.Co.Uk*. https://mobilesquared.co.uk/wp-content/uploads/2017/12/Conversational-Advertising.pdf.

“Why Is Mars Red?”. 2022. *Childrensmuseum.Org*. https://www.childrensmuseum.org/blog/why-mars-red.

“Which Metals Are The Heaviest?”. 2022. *Sciencing*. https://sciencing.com/metals-heaviest-8751708.html.

“Cardiovascular disease causes one-third of deaths worldwide.” 2022. *Science Daily*. https://www.sciencedaily.com/releases/2017/05/170517143625.htm

“Dots Don’t Matter In Gmail Addresses - Gmail Help”. 2022. *Support.Google.Com*. https://support.google.com/mail/answer/7436150?hl=en.

“Jiffy (Time) - Wikipedia”. 2022. *En.Wikipedia.Org*. https://en.wikipedia.org/wiki/Jiffy_(time).

"Human Body Farm Research Uncovers 'Astounding' Movement Of Dead Arms". 2019. *Abc.Net.Au.* https://www.abc.net.au/news/2019-09-12/dead-bodies-move-while-decomposing-significant-find-for-police/11492330.

"Gli "Amanti Di Modena" Erano Due Individui Di Sesso Maschile". 2019. *Magazine*.Unibo.It. https://magazine.unibo.it/archivio/2019/09/11/gli-201camanti-di-modena201d-erano-due-individui-di-sesso-maschile.

Maisano, Jessica A., Travis J. Laduc, Christopher J. Bell, and Diane Barber. 2019. **"The Cephalic Osteoderms Of Varanus Komodoensis As Revealed By High Resolution X-Ray Computed Tomography"**. *The Anatomical Record 302 (10)*: 1675-1680. doi:10.1002/ar.24197.

"Matryoshka Diamond Found In Yakutia | Alrosa". 2022. *Eng.Alrosa.Ru.* http://eng.alrosa.ru/58808/.

"Behavioural Laterality In Foraging Bottlenose Dolphins (Tursiops Truncatus) | Royal Society Open Science". 2022. *Royal Society Open Science.* https://royalsocietypublishing.org/doi/10.1098/rsos.190929.

Baskota, Anuj, Seungho Kim, Hosung Kang, and Sunghwan Jung. 2019. **"Acceleration-Induced Water Ejection In The Human Ear Canal"**. *Bulletin Of The American Physical Society Volume 64, Number 13.* https://meetings.aps.org/Meeting/DFD19/Session/A31.7.

Castles, Madelaine P., Rachel Brand, Alecia J. Carter, Martine Maron, Kerryn D. Carter, and Anne W. Goldizen. 2019. **"Relationships Between Male Giraffes' Colour, Age And Sociability"**. *Animal Behaviour 157: 13-25.* doi:10.1016/j.anbehav.2019.08.003.

"Hiccups - Symptoms And Causes". 2022. Mayo Clinic. https://www.mayoclinic.org/diseases-conditions/hiccups/symptoms-causes/syc-20352613.

Khattak, Hamza K., Pablo Bianucci, and Aaron D. Slepkov. 2019. **"Linking Plasma Formation In Grapes To Microwave Resonances Of Aqueous Dimers"**. *Proceedings Of The National Academy Of Sciences 116 (10): 4000-4005.* doi:10.1073/pnas.1818350116.

"Do Intelligent People Have More Zinc And Copper In Their Hair? | Did You Know It?". 2008. *Did You Know It?.* http://www.didyouknow.it/2008/11/27/intelligent-people-have-more-zinc-and-copper-in-their-hair/.

"Universe Forum--Black Holes--What Are They?". 2022. *Lweb.Cfa.Harvard.Edu.* https://lweb.cfa.harvard.edu/seuforum/bh_whatare.htm.

“What Really Happens When Lightning Strikes Sand”. 2022. *Discover Magazine.* https://www.discovermagazine.com/the-sciences/what-really-happens-when-lightning-strikes-sand-the-science-behind-a-viral-photo.

HowStuffWorks, Science, Science, and Production. 2012. **“How Much Energy In A Hurricane, A Volcano, And An Earthquake?”**. *Howstuffworks.* https://science.howstuffworks.com/environmental/energy/energy-hurricane-volcano-earthquake1.htm

Purtill, Corinne. 2018. **“An Astronaut Explains Why You Can’T Burp In Space”.** *Quartz.* https://qz.com/1449587/can-you-burp-in-space/.

Mukherjee, Mithu. 2014. **“In Zero Gravity, A Candle’s Flame Is Round And Blue! - Save Our Green”.** *Save Our Green.* https://saveourgreen.org/allpost/in-zero-gravity-a-candles-flame-is-round-and-blue/.

“Your Body Is A Planet”. 2022. *Discover Magazine.* https://www.discovermagazine.com/health/your-body-is-a-planet.

“NPR Cookie Consent And Choices”. 2022. *Npr.Org.* https://www.npr.org/sections/goatsandsoda/2015/04/06/397879410/go-ahead-little-goat-eat-some-poison-ivy-it-wont-hurt-a-bit?t=1578658197234.

“NPR Cookie Consent And Choices”. 2022. *Npr.Org.* https://www.npr.org/sections/krulwich/2010/07/01/128170775/a-very-scary-light-show-exploding-h-bombs-in-space.

Republic, Food. 2013. **“14 Things You Didn’t Know About Strawberries - Food Republic”.** *Food Republic.* https://www.foodrepublic.com/2013/05/20/14-things-you-didnt-know-about-strawberries/.

“What To Do If You’ve Found A Bat - Bat World Sanctuary”. 2022. *Bat World Sanctuary.* https://batworld.org/what-to-do-if-you-found_a_bat/.

“8 Birds That Can’T Fly”. 2022. *Encyclopedia Britannica.* https://www.britannica.com/list/8-birds-that-cant-fly.

“Horizon Magazine”. 2022. Ec.Europa.Eu. https://ec.europa.eu/research-and-innovation/en/horizon-magazine.

“ UCSB Science Line”. 2022. *Scienceline.Ucsb.Edu.* http://scienceline.ucsb.edu/getkey.php?key=4831.

“The New Plastics Economy: Catalysing Action”. 2022. *Ellenmacarthurfoundation.Org.* https://ellenmacarthurfoundation.org/the-new-plastics-economy-catalysing-action.

"What Part Of The Bathroom Can You Clean With This?". 2013. *Huffpost UK*. https://www.huffpost.com/entry/clean-a-toilet-bowl-gatorade_n_2451993.

"Why Hot Water Freezes Faster Than Cold—Physicists Solve The Mpemba Effect". 2013. *Medium*. https://medium.com/the-physics-arxiv-blog/why-hot-water-freezes-faster-than-cold-physicists-solve-the-mpemba-effect-d8a2f611e853.

"The Dvorak Keyboard". 2022. *Mit.Edu*. http://www.mit.edu/~jcb/Dvorak/.

Health, Brain, Why Universe, and BrainMD Life. 2016. **"Why Your Brain Is Like The Universe | Brainmd Life"**. *Brainmd Health Blog*. https://brainmd.com/blog/how-your-brain-is-like-the-universe/#.

Ann, Leslie, and Leslie Ann. 2012. **"It's Corny, But It's REALLY Yummy"**. *WZOZ 103.1*. https://wzozfm.com/its-corny-but-its-really-yummy/.

HowStuffWorks, Health, Body, and Parts. 2007. **"16 Unusual Facts About The Human Body"**. *Howstuffworks*. https://health.howstuffworks.com/human-body/parts/16-unusual-facts-about-the-human-body.htm#pt

Author, More. 2015. **"Can All Of Mankind Fit Inside A Sugar Cube?"**. *Science ABC*. https://www.scienceabc.com/pure-sciences/can-the-entire-human-race-fit-inside-a-sugar-cube.html.

"Alien Hand Syndrome - Wikipedia". 2015. *En.Wikipedia.Org*. https://en.wikipedia.org/wiki/Alien_hand_syndrome.

"Bee Gees Song Stayin' Alive Helps Doctors Perform CPR". *The Telegraph*. https://www.telegraph.co.uk/news/worldnews/northamerica/usa/3214030/Bee-Gees-song-Stayin-Alive-helps-doctors-perform-CPR.html.

"The Drugs Derived From Deadly Poisons". 2013. *BBC News*. https://www.bbc.com/news/magazine-24551945.

"Thunderstorm Numbers Calculated". 2022. *BBC News*. https://www.bbc.com/news/science-environment-12991483.

"What Is The Strongest Muscle In The Human Body?". *2022. The Library Of Congress*. https://www.loc.gov/everyday-mysteries/item/what-is-the-strongest-muscle-in-the-human-body/.
"How Many Molecules Are In A Drop Of Water?". 2022. *Thoughtco*. https://www.thoughtco.com/atoms-in-a-drop-of-water-609425.

van Dongen, Eelco V., Ingrid H.P. Kersten, Isabella C. Wagner, Richard G.M. Morris, and Guillén Fernández. 2016. **"Physical Exercise Performed Four Hours After Learning Improves Memory Retention And Increases Hippocampal Pattern Similarity During Retrieval"**. *Current Biology 26 (13): 1722-1727. doi:10.1016/j.cub.2016.04.071.*

Harding, Dr. 2018. **"Sweaty Feet | Why Do My Feet Sweat? | Treatment"**. *Patient.Info.* https://patient.info/skin-conditions/excessive-sweating-hyperhidrosis/sweaty-feet.

"Hairy Ball Theorem - Wikipedia". 2022. *En.Wikipedia.Org.* https://en.wikipedia.org/wiki/Hairy_ball_theorem.

Apanga, Paschal Awingura, John Koku Awoonor-Williams, Michael Acheampong, and Matthew Ayamba Adam. 2016. **"A Presumptive Case Of Human Rabies: A Rare Survived Case In Rural Ghana"**. *Frontiers In Public Health 4.* doi:10.3389/fpubh.2016.00256.

HowStuffWorks, Science, Science, Mind, and Emotions. 2009. **"How Many Muscles Does It Take To Smile?"**. *Howstuffworks.* https://science.howstuffworks.com/life/inside-the-mind/emotions/muscles-smile.htm.

HowStuffWorks, Science, Science, and Optics. 2007. **"How Holograms Work"**. *Howstuffworks.* https://science.howstuffworks.com/hologram.htm.

"Pratfall Effect - Wikipedia". 2022. *En.Wikipedia.Org.* https://en.wikipedia.org/wiki/Pratfall_effect.

"Does Cold Weather Make You Sick: What's The Link?". 2022. *Medicalnewstoday.Com.* https://www.medicalnewstoday.com/articles/323431#cold-weather-and-viruses.

"Girls Have Superior Sense of Taste To Boys." 2008. *Science Daily.* https://www.sciencedaily.com/releases/2008/12/081216104035.htm

Shipman, Matt. 2018. **"How Big Can Snowflakes Be?"**. *NC State News.* https://news.ncsu.edu/2018/12/how-big-can-snowflakes-be/.

"Wednesday Wisdom: Your Body Has Enough Of This To Produce Over 7 Bars Of Soap?". 2018. *Soma Tech Intl's Blog.* https://www.somatechnology.com/blog/wednesday-wisdom/wednesday-wisdom-your-body-has-enough-of-this-to-produce-over-7-bars-of-soap/.

"Dusting The Virtues Of Snow". 2013. *Earthobservatory.Nasa.Gov.* https://earthobservatory.nasa.gov/features/DirtySnow.

"What do babies dream about in the womb." 2022. https://www.eqdiapers.com.ph/good_reads/what-do-babies-dream-about-in-the-womb.

"Worm Facts | The Adventures Of Herman The Worm | U Of I Extension". 2022. *Web.Extension.Illinois.Edu.* https://web.extension.illinois.edu/worms/facts/.

"Facts About Great White Sharks". 2014. *Livescience.Com.* https://www.livescience.com/27338-great-white-sharks.html.

"Water Integrator - Wikipedia". 2022. *En.Wikipedia.Org.* https://en.wikipedia.org/wiki/Water_integrator.

"How Honey Heals Wounds". 2022. *Science Learning Hub.* https://www.sciencelearn.org.nz/resources/1702-how-honey-heals-wounds.

"Why Can't You Hold Your Breath Until You're Dead? | Evolutionary Psychology Blog Archive". 2022. *Web.Sas.Upenn.Edu.* https://web.sas.upenn.edu/kurzbanepblog/2011/02/07/why-cant-you-hold-your-breath-until-youre-dead/.

"Women In Computing - Wikipedia". 2022. *En.Wikipedia.Org.* https://en.wikipedia.org/wiki/Women_in_computing.

"Newfoundland And Labrador Iceberg Facts". 2022. *Newfoundland And Labrador, Canada – Official Tourism Website.* https://www.newfoundlandlabrador.com/trip-ideas/travel-stories/iceberg-facts.

"Steam Engine - Definition, Etymology And Usage, Examples And Related Words". 2022. Finedictionary.Com. http://www.finedictionary.com/steam%20engine.html.

Nast, Condé. 2022. "A Lab-Grown-Meat Startup Gets The FDA'S Stamp Of Approval". WIRED UK. https://www.wired.co.uk/article/lab-grown-meat-approval. australian-scientists-discover-500-meter-tall-coral-reef-in-the-great-barrier-reef-first-to-be-discovered-in-over-120-years/.

"New Gadget Could Reduce Shark Bycatch By 90%". 2022. The Guardian. https://www.theguardian.com/environment/2022/nov/21/new-gadget-could-reduce-shark-bycatch-by-90.

"Hair Follicles Grown In The Lab In A Step Towards Hair Loss Treatment". 2023. New Scientist. https://www.newscientist.com/article/2343357-hair-follicles-grown-in-the-lab-in-a-step-towards-hair-loss-treatment/.

"Best Of The Brink 2022: 10 Amazing Discoveries And Mind-Blowing Facts". 2023. Boston University. https://www.bu.edu/articles/2022/10-amazing-discoveries-and-science-facts-of-2022/.

Animals & Nature

There's no doubt that 2023 was a year where 'going green' went from cool to crucial. And in 2024, climate change and environmental conservation continue to make headlines around the world, pushing us to rethink our relationship with the planet. It's a call to action, prompting us to appreciate and protect the intricate web of life that surrounds us.

Right in our own backyard, we share space with an array of incredible plants and animals. There are orchids outsmarting insects to aid their survival, and birds charting epic migratory routes with precision. Each species, no matter how great or small, weaves its own unique thread into the rich tapestry of life on Earth.

In this chapter, we have found some of the most fascinating facts about our planet and the creatures that call it home.

The summer of 2022 saw Europe's worst drought in 500 years, with extreme heat warnings affecting two-thirds of the continent.

• • •

In 2023, researchers from Waseda University in Tokyo detected microplastics in clouds above Mount Fuji for the first time, which they believe came from the ocean.

• • •

A lamb can identify its mother by her bleating sound.

• • •

Spider web silk is stronger than steel.

Icebergs can weigh more than 10 million tonnes.

• • •

Bees have teeth. Not quite in the same way as mammals, but they have narrow, rounded points on their mandibles (jaws).

• • •

In 2023, a Category 5 storm, with winds surpassing 157 miles per hour (252 km/h), occurred in every ocean basin worldwide for the first time in recorded history.

• • •

Penguins and ostriches are the only birds that can swim, but not fly.

Beavers were given legal protection in England in 2022, 400 years after they were hunted to extinction. It is now illegal to trap, injure, kill or disturb beavers, as they are officially recognised as native wildlife by the government.

• • •

The HPAI H5N1 virus, a highly lethal bird flu variant, was identified in bird and seal populations on Antarctica's Bird Island in October 2023, raising concerns over the potential threat to native wildlife.

• • •

Cats can be allergic to the perfumes and scents that humans use.

When you sneeze, air comes out of your nose at around 100 mph (160 km/h).

• • •

In 2023, Louisiana embarked on the single-largest ecosystem restoration project in U.S. history by reconnecting the Mississippi River with its wetlands

• • •

Rain has a real smell, which was named 'petrichor' by Australian scientists in 1964. It is a mixture of plant oils, bacteria, and ozone.

• • •

How come we can always find room for dessert after a large meal? It's called sensory-specific satiety. This means that the body has different limits for different types of food. This is also the reason why the last piece of pizza never tastes as good as the first!

From November 2022 to October 2023, Earth experienced its hottest 12-month period on record, with temperatures rising 2.3 degrees Fahrenheit (1.3 degrees Celsius) above preindustrial levels, nearing the critical 2.7 degrees Fahrenheit (1.5 degrees Celsius) benchmark of the 2015 Paris Agreement.

• • •

Think that clouds are light and fluffy? Think again! A single cloud can weigh 453 tonnes (1.1 million lbs).

• • •

Termites are the longest living insects. They can live for up to 100 years.

• • •

Squirrels are one of the most common causes of power outages in the US.

In 2022, researchers documented the rare black-necked pheasant pigeon for the first time in 140 years. This ground-dwelling bird species, found only in the deep forests of Papua New Guinea, was previously believed to be extinct.

• • •

A single bat can consume up to 1,000 mosquitoes in one hour.

• • •

The most common wild bird in the world is the red-billed quelea, which live in Africa and have an estimated population of 1.5 billion.

• • •

Jupiter was recognised for having the most moons in our solar system with 95 moons verified in February 2023, before Saturn quickly stole the title by May with 146 verified moons.

The platypus doesn't have a stomach: their oesophagus goes straight to their intestines.

• • •

Some spiders can make milk for their babies.

• • •

Spiders have transparent blood. The colourless blood is called hemolymph.

• • •

The children of identical twins are genetically half-siblings, not cousins. They share 25% of the same DNA, as opposed to the 12.5% that cousins share.

For every 0.45kg (1 pound) of fat gained, you add seven miles (11.26 km) of new blood vessels.

• • •

The 2022 volcanic eruption in Tonga was identified in June 2023 as producing the most intense lightning ever observed, with a "supercharged" thunderstorm generating nearly 200,000 lightning flashes, peaking at over 2600 bolts per minute.

• • •

Giraffes that have dark spots are more dominant than those with light spots.

Researchers in Costa Rica found that if you spread the leftover pulp from coffee production over the land, trees will grow four times as fast.

• • •

The world's largest cave is the Son Doong Cave in "Eudyptula wilsonae," a new extinct species of penguin was discovered in 2023. It became the oldest-known extinct little penguin, and shares ancestry with New Zealand's little penguins/kororā.

• • •

Octopuses have three hearts.

To save the declining rhino population at Kaziranga National Park in India, park rangers were given permission to shoot poachers. The park's rhino population had grown to 2,400 by 2017, making up two-thirds of the world's rhino population. Rangers estimate that around 20 poachers are shot at the park each year, and in 2015 more poachers were killed by rangers than rhinos killed by poachers.

• • •

We have no muscles in our fingers. Their movements are controlled by muscles in the palms and arms.

In 2023, authorities in Lake Tahoe, California, discovered that the break-ins attributed to Hank the Tank, a male black bear, were actually perpetrated by three bears, with a female bear, 64F, responsible for the majority. They had been on the run for a year before they were captured and rehomed at the Wild Animal Sanctuary in Colorado.

• • •

In the polar caps and many alpine areas worldwide, scientists have discovered pink snow that smells exactly like fresh watermelon. It is caused by a type of green algae that contains a red pigment. However tempting it may sound, they warn that eating it may cause diarrhoea.

• • •

Your body gives off enough heat in half an hour to be able to boil a gallon (4l) of water.

Sorry to break it to you, but spiders don't only live on land! In fact, sea spiders can have a leg span of over one foot (30 cm). During a 2023 expedition, scientists witnessed them mating for the first time. There's even a video.

• • •

Although no one has ever witnessed it, spiders are capable of farting.

• • •

By area, the United Kingdom has more tornadoes per year than anywhere else in the world.

• • •

The official bird of Redondo Beach, California is the Goodyear Blimp.

Tree rings grow wider in years when the weather is warm and wet.

• • •

The bigger the brain of an animal, the longer it will yawn. Mice have short yawns, while dogs, camels, and humans have the longest yawns.

• • •

One bolt of lightning has enough energy to toast 100,000 pieces of bread.

• • •

It takes 1,000 years for the average piece of plastic to break down. Even then, it will just break down into smaller pieces of plastic.

Robert Fedrock found the world's tallest poison ivy plant in Paris, Ontario, Canada, in 2023, measuring 68 feet tall, equivalent to the height of two stacked school buses. He suffered from a poison ivy rash, but gained local fame.

• • •

The world's largest freshwater fish is the Beluga Sturgeon; it can grow up to 20 feet long and live up to 100 years.

• • •

Cats were never mentioned in the Bible.

Ticks can be a human's worst nightmare. And to make matters worse, a 2023 study revealed that ticks can travel through the air via static electricity, meaning they can attach to your skin without the need to crawl.

• • •

Squirrels and other rodents have continuously growing front teeth, kept at a manageable length by constantly gnawing on nuts. These teeth grow at an approximate rate of 6 inches per year.

• • •

It is believed that dinosaurs may have shed their skin in chunks, rather than all at once like modern reptiles.

There is a fruit in Central and South America called black sapote that tastes like chocolate pudding.

• • •

Research from the University of North Florida in 2023 found significant dietary differences in alligators living on golf courses compared to those in natural habitats, including unusual items like canned corn and a cheeseburger with fries.

• • •

Cats can recognise their names, but they can also choose to ignore them when they want to.

• • •

Between 1993 and 2010, the Earth tilted 31.5 inches to the east, a shift attributed to the extensive pumping of groundwater, as discovered in 2023.

A tiny breed of shark was discovered in 2015 (but only recognised as a new species in 2019). It is only 5.5 cm in length and looks like a miniature sperm whale.

• • •

Between 1970 and 2018 wildlife population sizes decreased by 68% worldwide.

• • •

There is a type of psychoactive fungus that can make cicada butts fall off when they come into contact with it.

• • •

Only female mosquitoes bite because they need protein from blood to help their eggs develop.

In 2023, we discovered that rats like to be tickled. Scientists tickled rats to study brain regions responsible for laughter and playfulness, and it turns out they liked it.

• • •

Carrots used to be purple, yellow and white — but not orange.

• • •

Sharks are older than trees, according to *Smithsonian* magazine. The oldest species of trees existed around 350 million years ago in the Sahara desert, while sharks have been around for over 400 million years.

The weight of a cow can vary by 34kg (75 lb) in one day.

• • •

Currently, there are over one million animal species that are close to extinction—more than ever before.

• • •

The Pacific Ocean is gradually shrinking, with North and South America moving westward by 2-3 centimeters per year, a geological shift observed in 2023.

• • •

Ducks can see ultraviolet light.

In 2017 and 2019, green coloured puppies were born. However, this was due to bile pigment in the womb and it eventually faded.

• • •

In 2020, scientists discovered evidence of cancer in a dinosaur bone for the first time.

• • •

Nearly 10 horses die every week on American race tracks, more than any other country in the world.

• • •

Bed bugs were around at the same time as the dinosaurs. Unfortunately, they survived the extinction.

The brains of some tiny spiders overflow into their legs.

• • •

Female kangaroos have three vaginas.

• • •

Some species of squid can shoot out a cloud of black ink to help them escape predators, the ink cloud is made of a mixture of ink and seawater, and it can change colour and texture to help them blend in with the background.

• • •

According to a 2023 report, 48% of species are declining and on their way to extinction, with the extinction rate currently 1,000 times the natural rate.

In mid-March 2022, a colossal collapse happened on the Conger ice shelf, the first time such a collapse has been recorded in the eastern part of Antarctica since satellite observations began in 1979. The collapse of the ice shelf, which covers an area of 450 square miles (1165.49 sq. km), occurred earlier than predicted by experts and in a region of the continent that is believed to be less susceptible to the impacts of climate change.

•••

In one season, a single seahorse can produce over 2,000 babies; and it's the males that give birth, not the females.

•••

Flamingos get their pink colour from their food. They eat tiny blue-green algae and shrimp that turn pink during digestion.

The world's largest spider is the Goliath birdeater tarantula, and can have a leg span of up to 11 inches.

•••

There are no male and female earthworms; they all have male and female body parts.

•••

Jellyfish evaporate in the sun. They are 98 per cent water.

•••

Within the next 2 decades, global temperatures are likely to reach 1.5 degrees Celsius above pre-industrial levels, the so-called "tipping point" of climate change.

A full bladder is about the size of a softball.

• • •

A small blue fruit that grows in parts of Africa is the world's most intense natural colour.

• • •

Churchill, Manitoba, in Canada, known as the polar bear capital of the world, has implemented safety strategies to protect citizens from polar bear encounters. In 2000, the town closed the open-air dump to keep bears from entering the town for food. Citizens are advised to leave their doors unlocked for emergency refuge in case of a bear encounter.

More than 90 per cent of greenhouse gases being trapped by the Earth are stored in the oceans.

• • •

Data shows that 3 million heat pump units installed in Europe in 2022 replaced around 4 billion cubic meters of natural gas, avoiding 8 million tonnes of CO2 emissions.

• • •

During solar eclipses, bees stop buzzing.

• • •

Renewable energy is becoming the world's top source of electricity. According to the International Energy Agency, 90% of new electricity demand between now and 2025 will be covered by clean energy sources like wind and solar, along with nuclear energy.

Human birth control pills work on gorillas.

• • •

If a starfish is divided into five pieces, as long as each part has some of the central disc still attached, five new starfish will form.

• • •

A zebra is black with white stripes.

• • •

The world's largest amphibian is the Chinese giant salamander, which can reach up to 5.9 feet long and weigh up to 6.8 kg (140 lb.)

• • •

A bat's teeth are so sharp that its victims may feel no bite, and its saliva helps to numb any pain while sucking blood.

In a study, pigeons were able to learn all the letters of the alphabet.

• • •

Tigers have striped skin.

• • •

The world's largest flower is not found on land, but in the ocean. The *rafflesia arnoldii* can reach up to 91 cm (3 feet) in diameter and weigh up to 15 pounds.

• • •

The *mimosa pudica*, an exotic herb from South and Central America can learn and remember things as well as many animals.

Bison are the largest land mammals in North America.

• • •

Elephants have their own alarm call, which means ‘humans’.

• • •

There are approximately 8.7 million species of animals and 391,000 species of plants on Earth.

• • •

Fleas can jump to a height of up to 60 times their body length.

Satellite data shows that deforestation in the Brazilian Amazon in January 2023 was down 61% compared to the previous year, after the election of President Lula who has pledged to protect the rainforest.

• • •

SharkGuard, a battery-powered device released in 2022, keeps sharks and rays safe from being unintentionally trapped in commercial fishing nets by emitting a short electrical pulse every few seconds, causing them to swim away unharmed.

• • •

Azara's owl monkeys are more monogamous than humans.

The legs of a Tyrannosaurus Rex were about 3.6 m (12 feet) long. Its arms were only 90 cm (3 feet long).

• • •

Castoreum is an anal secretion that beavers use to mark their territories. It smells like vanilla and is used in food and perfume, often labelled as a natural flavouring.

• • •

The reason our fingers get wrinkly when left in water is the body's way of helping us have a better grip on wet objects.

The Coronavirus (and other viruses) can't harm bats.

• • •

Reindeer eyeballs turn blue in winter to help them see at lower light levels.

• • •

Owls don't have eyeballs. They have eye tubes.

• • •

The Saharan silver ant is the world's fastest ant, and it can run at one meter per second on the desert sand.

Sloths can hold their breath underwater for 40 minutes.

• • •

In 2022, researchers found that trees at the edge of forests grow faster than the ones in the middle.

• • •

Mosquitoes are attracted to the colour blue twice as much as any other colour.

• • •

Giraffes have one of the highest blood pressures of all animals due to the distance between their head and heart.

Wombat poop is in the shape of a cube. This is because of the way the intestines produce the faeces. Wombats will then stack these cubes to mark their territory.

•••

The world's largest living organism is the armillaria ostoyae, a fungus that covers 2,200 acres in Oregon.

•••

If an octopus is scared or angry, it can turn a different colour.

•••

Teeth start growing about six months before you're born, they're just not visible for around 6-12 months.

Apples can wake you up better than coffee, as they contain 13g of natural sugar.

• • •

The 20 warmest years ever on record have all been in the last 22 years.

• • •

Some catfish can kill pigeons.

• • •

The world's largest volcanic eruption in recorded history was the eruption of Tambora in Indonesia in 1815, which killed over 92,000 people.

If all the land glaciers in the world were to melt, the water they would release could raise ocean levels by more than 70 m.

• • •

Moths can't fly during an earthquake.

• • •

A fetus in the womb can get hiccups.

• • •

You are taller in the morning — the cartilage between your bones compresses throughout the day, meaning you can be up to 1 cm (0.39 in) shorter at the end of the day.

On a pound-for-pound basis, human babies are stronger than oxen.

• • •

Clownfish start off as males and develop into females later on in life.

• • •

Kittens sleep so much because a growth hormone is released only while they are sleeping.

• • •

Recycling a three-foot stack of newspapers can save a whole tree.

Butterflies need to have a body temperature lower than 27.7°C (82°F) to be able to fly.

• • •

House flies have a lifespan of between two weeks and a month.

• • •

When a male donkey and a female horse mate, the offspring are called mules. However, when a male horse and a female donkey mate, the offspring are called hinnies.

• • •

Cats will rarely meow at another cat. Cats use this sound for humans.

Dogs can learn words. A Border Collie named Rico learnt 200 different objects by name.

• • •

It would take 1,200,000 mosquitoes, each sucking once, to completely drain the average human of blood.

• • •

You're more likely to be killed by a dog or a cow than a shark.

• • •

Rhino horns are worth about US$9,000 per pound (0.45kg) in Asia, which is what fuels the poaching trade in Africa.

When the moon is directly over your head you weigh slightly less.

• • •

The world's most common disease is tooth decay.

• • •

Apes suffer from midlife crises just like humans do.

• • •

Skin is our largest organ.

• • •

A mantis shrimp can swing its claw so fast it boils the water around it and creates a flash of light.

To know when to mate, a male giraffe will continuously headbutt the female in the bladder until she urinates. The male then tastes the urine and that helps him determine whether the female is ovulating.

• • •

Elephants can be pregnant for up to two years.

• • •

Honey is the only food that doesn't spoil.

• • •

Alpacas can get sick or die from loneliness, so it is always best to keep them in pairs, or bigger groups.

Kangaroos use their tails as a third leg. This is called the ‘tripod stance’.

• • •

You can see Australia’s Great Barrier Reef from space.

• • •

A hummingbird visits an average of 1,000 flowers a day for nectar.

• • •

The blood of mammals is red, the blood of insects is yellow, and the blood of lobsters is blue (it is clear, but turns blue in contact with oxygen).

The nail of your middle finger grows the fastest, and your thumbnail grows the slowest.

• • •

If you plant an apple seed it is almost guaranteed to grow a tree of a different type of apple.

• • •

A study found that pigs are on the same intellectual level as chimpanzees.

• • •

A group of frogs is called an army.

Two-thirds of the world's polar bears live in Canada.

• • •

Camels can drink 240 litres (53 gallons) of water in just three minutes.

• • •

Camel milk does not curdle.

• • •

Tigers might be known as great hunters, but in fact, only 10 per cent of their hunts end successfully.

• • •

Outbreaks of the bubonic plague (the Black Death) still occur around the world today.

A hummingbird weighs less than a penny.

• • •

A dolphin's blowhole is an evolved nose that is positioned at the top of their head.

• • •

The saliva of a chameleon is 400 times thicker than human saliva.

• • •

Cast iron cookware can leach iron into our food, making it great for anemics.

• • •

A 49 million-year-old cockroach fossil was found in 2014.

A blue whale's heart is as large as a small car, and you can hear it beat from two miles (3.2 km) away.

• • •

Owls cannot move their eyeballs.

• • •

Dogs and humans are the only animals with prostates.

• • •

Male turkeys are called gobblers.

• • •

There are over 2,000 species of starfish.

Birds fly in a ‘v’ formation to save energy.

• • •

Female glowworms use their luminous tails to attract mates.

• • •

As they turn into moths, caterpillars almost completely liquify.

• • •

The tongue of a blue whale can weigh as much as an elephant.

A 15-year-old cat has probably spent about 10 years of its life sleeping.

• • •

Bees have five eyes.

• • •

In the winter, camels can survive six or seven months without drinking any water.

• • •

If a lobster loses an appendage, it can grow another one.

• • •

The urine of a maned wolf smells like marijuana.

More than four million hectares of forest are lost every year in Africa.

• • •

The human brain is about 60 per cent fat, making it the fattiest organ in the body.

• • •

During the last ice age, beavers that were 2.4 m (8 ft) long roamed the Earth.

• • •

Bamboo can grow up to 9.1 m (36 in) in a single day.

Dogs watch more television now than a few years ago because modern televisions flicker at a speed that dogs are now able to process.

• • •

A Russian man grew a 5 cm (2 in) fir tree in his lung. He thought it was a cancerous tumour, but surgeons found the tree when operating.

• • •

Stingrays can jump out of the water.

• • •

Horned toads can shoot blood from their eyeballs.

Every night, we sleep with up to 10 million mites in the bed.

• • •

Babies are born without kneecaps. Kneecaps develop around the age of four.

• • •

The pistol shrimp, which is only about 2cm (0.78 in) in length, holds the title for the world's loudest animal. This tiny crustacean can snap its claw with such velocity that it generates a bubble. When this bubble collapses, it emits a sonic blast surpassing the loudness of a Concorde's sonic boom.

Sources

Wang, Y., Okochi, H., Tani, Y., Hayami, H., Minami, Y., Katsumi, N., ... & Niida, Y. (2023). *Environmental Chemistry Letters,* 21(6), 3055-3062. https://doi.org/10.1007/s10311-023-01626-x.

Mersereau, D. (2024). "A World First, Every Tropical Ocean Saw A Category 5 Storm In 2023". *Theweathernetwork.com.* https://www.theweathernetwork.com/en/news/weather/severe/a-world-first-every-tropical-ocean-saw-a-category-5-hurricane-cyclone-in-2023.

"First Confirmed Cases Of Avian Influenza In The Antarctic Region". 2023. *Bas.ac.uk.* https://www.bas.ac.uk/media-post/first-confirmed-cases-of-avian-influenza-in-the-antarctic-region/.

"Earth's Hottest 12-Month Streak". N.d. *Climatecentral.org.* https://www.climatecentral.org/climate-matters/earths-hottest-12-month-streak-2023.

"O'Callaghan, J. (2023). 'With 62 Newly Discovered Moons, Saturn Knocks Jupiter Off Its Pedestal". *Nytimes.com.* https://www.nytimes.com/2023/05/12/science/saturn-moons-jupiter.html.

"Global Volcanism Program: Hunga Tonga-Hunga Ha'apai". N.d. *Volcano.si.edu.* https://volcano.si.edu/volcano.cfm?vn=243040.

Magazine, S. (2023). "New Extinct Species Of "Ridiculously Cute," Tiny Penguins Discovered In New Zealand". *Smithsonianmag.com.* https://www.smithsonianmag.com/smart-news/new-extinct-species-of-ridiculously-cute-tiny-penguins-discovered-in-new-zealand-180982504/.

Rossen, J. (2023). "'Hank The Tank' Caught: Burglar Bear's Crime Spree Comes To An End-But With A Twist". *Mentalfloss.com.* https://www.mentalfloss.com/posts/hank-the-tank-lake-tahoe-bear-burglar.

"Video Captures Giant Sea Spiders Mating For The First Time'" N.d. *Earth.com.* https://www.earth.com/news/video-shows-giant-sea-spiders-mating-for-the-first-time/.

Rodriguez, A. (2023). "Man Has A Rash Of Good Luck When He Discovers Tallest Poison Ivy Plant". *Guinnessworldrecords.com.* https://www.guinnessworldrecords.com/news/2023/6/man-has-a-rash-of-good-luck-when-he-discovers-tallest-poison-ivy-plant-750701.

Rossen, J. (2023). "A Little-Known Tick Trick Allows Them To "Jump" Onto Your Skin". *Mentalfloss.com.* https://www.mentalfloss.com/posts/ticks-jump-using-static-electricity.

X, S. (2023). "Study Shows Life Near The Golf Course Isn't Easy For Alligators". *Phys.Org.* https://phys.org/news/2023-09-life-golf-isnt-easy-alligators.html.

Dzombak, R. (2023). "We've Pumped So Much Groundwater That We've Nudged The Earth's Spin, Says New Study". *Phys.org.* https://phys.org/news/2023-06-weve-groundwater-nudged-earth.html.

Golembiewski, K. (2023). "Scientists Tickle Rats To Learn About Brain Activity During Play". *Edition.cnn.com.* https://edition.cnn.com/2023/08/05/world/tickle-rats-play-brain-study-scn/index.html.

Earthday.Org. (2023). "5 Climate Change Facts To Scare You Into Action This Halloween". *Earthday.org.* https://www.earthday.org/5-terrifying-climate-change-facts-scare-halloween/.

Vernon, E. (2023). "10 Positive Climate News Stories From 2023 So Far". *Metrikus.io.* https://www.metrikus.io/blog/10-positive-climate-news-stories-from-2023.

"How And When Do Lambs Recognize The Bleats Of Their Mothers? | Bioacoustics Journal". 2022. *Bioacoustics.Info.* http://www.bioacoustics.info/article/how-and-when-do-lambs-recognize-bleats-their-mothers.

"The Spider Blood Circulation". 2022. *Ednieuw.Home.Xs4all.Nl.* https://ednieuw.home.xs4all.nl/Spiders/InfoNed/blood.html.

"Do Bees Have Teeth?". 2022. *Buzzaboutbees.Net.* https://www.buzzaboutbees.net/do-bees-have-teeth.html.

"List Of Animals In The Bible - Wikipedia". 2019. *En.Wikipedia.Org.* https://en.wikipedia.org/wiki/List_of_animals_in_the_Bible.

"Life On Plateau: Don't Eat The Algae That Smell Like Watermelon". 2019. *News.Cgtn.Com.* https://news.cgtn.com/news/3d3d514e3341444d32457a6333566d54/index.html.

"How Fast Is A Sneeze Versus A Cough? Cover Your Mouth Either Way!". 2022. *Lung.Org.* https://www.lung.org/blog/sneeze-versus-cough.

"Petrichor". 2022. *Acs.Org.* https://www.acs.org/content/dam/acsorg/education/students/highschool/chemistryclubs/infographics/petrichor-the-smell-of-rain.pdf.

"The Beach Reporter – Daily Breeze". 2022. *Daily Breeze*. https://www.dailybreeze.com/the-beach-reporter/.

"Spider Silk." 2022. *Science Daily*. https://www.sciencedaily.com/releases/2006/10/061009031730.htm

"The Blue Whales Heart | Size, Weight, Blood Vessels And Other Facts - WHALE FACTS". *WHALE FACTS. 2021*. https://www.whalefacts.org/blue-whale-heart.

Gutiérrez, Marta, and Marta Gutiérrez. 2015. **"Why Do Only Female Mosquitoes Bite?"**. *Revista Mètode*. https://metode.org/metodes-whys-and-wherefores/why-do-only-female-mosquitoes-bite.html.

"Adorable Shark Fits In Your Hand, Looks Like A Mini Sperm Whale". 2019. *Livescience.Com*. https://www.livescience.com/65989-american-pocket-shark-new-species.html.
Boyce, Greg R., Emile Gluck-Thaler, Jason C. Slot, Jason E. Stajich, William J. Davis, Tim Y. James, and John R. Cooley et al. 2018. **"Psychoactive Plant- And Mushroom-Associated Alkaloids From Two Behavior Modifying Cicada Pathogens"**. doi:10.1101/375105.

"Animal Records". 2022. *Google Books*. https://books.google.co.uk/books?id=T3FEKopUFkUC&pg=PA235&lpg=PA235&dq=termite+queen+longest+living+100+years&source=bl&ots=7D_kYu-ZNz&sig=b0AhhqAwAXcFpA1UoYU4jnnF2v4&hl=en&sa=X&redir_esc=y#v=onepage&q=termite%20que&f=false.

"The Atmosphere And The Water Cycle | U.S. Geological Survey". 2022. *Usgs.Gov*. https://www.usgs.gov/special-topics/water-science-school/science/atmosphere-and-water-cycle?qt-science_center_objects=0#qt-science_center_objects.

"Defending Against Outages: Squirrel Tracker | American Public Power Association". 2017. *Publicpower.Org*. https://www.publicpower.org/blog/defending-against-outages-squirrel-tracker.

"Finger Anatomy." 2022. *Medicinenet.Com*. https://www.medicinenet.com/image-collection/finger_anatomy_picture/picture.htm.

"Have You Ever Wondered: Does It Fart?". 2018. *Hachette Books*. https://www.hachettebooks.com/themed-article/have-you-ever-wondered-does-it-fart/.

Wilkinson, Laura L., and Jeffrey M. Brunstrom. 2016. **"Sensory Specific Satiety: More Than 'Just' Habituation?"**. *Appetite* 103: 221-228. doi:10.1016/j.appet.2016.04.019.

"Perfumes and Pets". 2022. *Heartofthevalleyshelter.Org*. https://heartofthevalleyshelter.org/wp-content/uploads/2012/06/PerfumesandPets.pdf.

"How Much Toast Can A Lightning Bolt Make?". 2014. *Thenakedscientists.Com*. https://www.thenakedscientists.com/articles/questions/how-much-toast-can-lightning-bolt-make.

"The Longer The Yawn, The Bigger The Brain". 2021.*Utrecht University*. https://www.uu.nl/en/news/the-longer-the-yawn-the-bigger-the-brain.

Magazine, Smithsonian, and Joseph Stromberg. 2012. **"This African Fruit Produces The World'S Most Intense Natural Colour"**. *Smithsonian Magazine*. https://www.smithsonianmag.com/science-nature/this-african-fruit-produces-the-worlds-most-intense-natural-colour-30070457/.

"Robotic Milkers And An Automated Greenhouse: Inside A High-Tech Small Farm (Published 2019)". 2019. *Nytimes.Com*. https://www.nytimes.com/2019/01/13/technology/farm-technology-milkers-robots.html.

"A Bird's-Eye View". 2022. Ducks.Org. https://www.ducks.org/conservation/waterfowl-research-science/a-birds-eye-view.
"10 Awesome And Little-Known Facts About The Human Body". 2022. *Drbruceresnick.Com*. https://www.drbruceresnick.com/blog/47688-10-awesome-and-little-known-facts-about-the-human-body.

"Tornado Climatology - Wikipedia". 2021. *En.Wikipedia.Org*. https://en.wikipedia.org/wiki/Tornado_climatology.

"Diospyros Nigra - Wikipedia". 2022. *En.Wikipedia.Org*. https://en.wikipedia.org/wiki/Diospyros_nigra.

Saito, Atsuko, Kazutaka Shinozuka, Yuki Ito, and Toshikazu Hasegawa. 2019. **"Domestic Cats (Felis Catus) Discriminate Their Names From Other Words"**. *Scientific Reports* 9 (1). doi:10.1038/s41598-019-40616-4.

"Dinosaur Dandruff Reveals First Evidence Of Skin Shedding". 2022. *BBC News*. https://www.bbc.com/news/science-environment-44252455.

"Golden Retriever Gives Birth To A Green Puppy Named 'Mojito'". 2019. *Iflscience*. https://www.iflscience.com/plants-and-animals/golden-retriever-gives-birth-to-a-green-puppy-named-mojito/.

"A Forest On Caffeine'? How Coffee Can Help Forests Grow Faster". 2022. *Environment*. https://www.nationalgeographic.com/environment/article/forest-on-caffeine-how-coffee-helps-forests-grow-faster.

"Horse racing's uncomfortable truth." 2019. *Penn Live*. https://www.pennlive.com/news/2019/05/horse-racings-uncomfortable-truth-horses-die-at-a-rate-of-more-than-one-per-week-in-pa.html

"Bedbugs Survived The Dinosaur Extinction Event". 2022. *BBC News*. https://www.bbc.com/news/science-environment-48274090.

"Rico (Dog) - Wikipedia". 2009. *En.Wikipedia.Org*. https://en.wikipedia.org/wiki/Rico_(dog).

Stoller-Conrad, Jessica. 2022. **"Tree Rings Provide Snapshots Of Earth's Past Climate – Climate Change: Vital Signs Of The Planet"**. *NASA*. Climate Change: Vital Signs Of The Planet. https://climate.nasa.gov/news/2540/tree-rings-provide-snapshots-of-earths-past-climate/

"Rhino Poacher Killed By Elephant And Eaten By Lions, Officials Say (Published 2019)". 2019. *Nytimes.Com*. https://www.nytimes.com/2019/04/07/world/africa/south-africa-poacher-rhino-lions.html.

"The Catfish That Strands Itself To Kill Pigeons". 2012. *Discover Magazine*. https://www.discovermagazine.com/planet-earth/the-catfish-that-strands-itself-to-kill-pigeons#.Xcnlu5NKiqD.

"The Real Science Of Bringing Back The Dinosaurs". 2018. *Popular Mechanics*. https://www.popularmechanics.com/science/animals/a21622026/jurassic-world-how-to-clone-a-dinosaur/.

Magazine, Smithsonian, and Rachael Lallensack. 2018. **"Busy Bees Take A Break During Total Solar Eclipses"**. *Smithsonian Magazine*. https://www.smithsonianmag.com/science-nature/busy-bees-take-break-during-total-solar-eclipses-180970502/.

"Tiny Tyrannosaur Hints At How T. Rex Became King (Published 2019)". 2019. *Nytimes.Com*. https://www.nytimes.com/2019/02/21/science/tiny-tyrannosaur-fossil.html.

"Why Carrots Are Orange (And 5 Non-Orange Carrots To Grow In Your Garden)". 2022. *Treehugger*. https://www.treehugger.com/why-carrots-are-orange-and-non-orange-carrots-grow-your-garden-4858707.

"Tiny Spider Brains Overflow Into The Body, Legs". 2011. *Scitechdaily*. https://scitechdaily.com/tiny-spider-brains-overflow-into-the-body-legs/.

"Kangaroos Have Three Vaginas". 2022. *Discover Magazine*. https://www.discovermagazine.com/the-sciences/kangaroos-have-three-vaginas.

Ling, Thomas. 2021. **"Why Are Flamingos Pink?"**. *BBC Science Focus Magazine.* https://www.sciencefocus.com/nature/why-are-flamingos-pink/.

"Jellyfish Evaporate In The Sun". 2022. *Explore-Knowmore.Blogspot.Com.* http://explore-knowmore.blogspot.com/2014/01/jellyfish-evaporate-in-sun.html.

"Bladder - Simple English Wikipedia, The Free Encyclopedia". 2022. *Wikipedia.* https://simple.wikipedia.org/wiki/Bladder.

"Octopus - Wikipedia". 2022. *En.Wikipedia.Org.* https://en.wikipedia.org/wiki/Octopus.

"These Animals Spawn The Most Offspring In One Go". 2022. *Animals.* https://www.nationalgeographic.com/animals/article/animals-with-most-offspring-fish-eggs-reproduction.

"Research And Discoveries Articles - Uchicago Medicine". 2022. *Uchicagomedicine.Org.* https://www.uchicagomedicine.org/forefront/research-and-discoveries-articles.

"Pigeons Nesting, Mating And Feeding Habits With Photos". 2022. *Wild-Bird-Watching.Com.* https://www.wild-bird-watching.com/Pigeons.html.

"National Geographic | Disney Australia & New Zealand - Disney Australia". 2022. *Disney Australia.* https://www.disney.com.au/national-geographic.
"Do Elephants Make Alarm Call That Means 'Humans!'? | Earth | Earthsky". 2014.

"Earthsky | Updates On Your Cosmos And World." https://earthsky.org/earth/do-elephants-make-alarm-call-that-means-humans/.

Dasgupta, Shreya. 2016. **"How Many Plant Species Are There In The World? Scientists Now Have An Answer"**. *Mongabay Environmental News.* https://news.mongabay.com/2016/05/many-plants-world-scientists-may-now-answer/.

"Some Monkeys Are (Really) Monogamous". 2014. *Livescience.Com.* https://www.livescience.com/44791-monkeys-monogamy.html.

"Castoreum - Wikipedia". 2022. *En.Wikipedia.Org.* https://en.wikipedia.org/wiki/Castoreum.

Becky Summers, Nature magazine. 2013. **"Why Do Our Fingers And Toes Wrinkle During A Bath?"**. *Scientific American.* https://www.scientificamerican.com/article/why-do-our-fingers-and-toes-wrinkle-during-a-bath/.

"Do Babies Have Kneecaps And When Do Kneecaps Form?". 2022. *Healthline*. https://www.healthline.com/health/do-babies-have-kneecaps#kneecaps-at-birth.

"9 Amazing Owl Facts". 2022. *Treehugger*. https://www.treehugger.com/owl-facts-that-will-amaze-you-4863920.

"8 Awesome Things You Didn't Know About Sloths". 2022. *The Dodo*. https://www.thedodo.com/8-awesome-things-you-didnt-kno-668962865.html.

"Why Are Mosquitos Attracked To The Colour Blue Than More Than Any Other Colour – Iron Zone". 2022. *Ironj11.Imascientist.Org.Uk*. https://ironj11.imascientist.org.uk/question/why-are-mosquitos-attracked-to-the-colour-blue-than-more-than-any-other-colour.

"BBC - Earth News - 'Supercharged' Heart Pumps Blood Up A Giraffe's Neck". 2022. *News.Bbc.Co.Uk*. http://news.bbc.co.uk/earth/hi/earth_news/newsid_8368000/8368915.stm.

"Why Is Wombat Poop Cube-Shaped?". 2022. *Animals*. https://www.nationalgeographic.com/animals/article/wombat-poop-cube-why-is-it-square-shaped.

"Octopuses Change Colour When They Are Feeling Aggressive | Plants And Animals". 2022. *Labroots*. https://www.labroots.com/trending/plants-and-animals/2386/octopuses-change-colour-when-they-are-feeling-aggressive.

"Your Teeth (For Kids) - Nemours Kidshealth". 2022. *Kidshealth.Org*. https://kidshealth.org/en/kids/teeth.html.

"Are Apples Better Than Coffee?". 2015. *CCE Suffolk County Family Health & Wellness*. https://blogs.cornell.edu/ccesuffolkfhw/2015/07/02/are-apples-better-than-coffee/.
"Mystery Of Moth Flight Uncovered". 2007. *Livescience.Com*. https://www.livescience.com/4338-mystery-moth-flight-uncovered.html.

"Is It Normal For My Baby To Have Hiccups In The Womb? | Babycenter". 2022. *Babycenter*. https://www.babycenter.com/pregnancy/your-body/is-it-normal-for-my-baby-to-have-hiccups-in-the-womb_2647.

"Study Guide for The Human Body in Health & Disease", Linda Swisher, Kevin T. Patton, Gary A. Thibodeau

"The Human Odyssey: Navigating the Twelve Stages of Life". Thomas Armstrong

"A Scientifically Accurate 'Finding Nemo' Would Have Been Very Different". 2022. *Business Insider*. https://www.businessinsider.com/clownfish-sex-changes-and-finding-nemo-2013-8?IR=T.

"Why Recycle". 2022. *Mariettarecycling.Org*. http://mariettarecycling.org/why.php.

HowStuffWorks, Animals, Animals, Arachnids, and Insects. 2008. **"How Butterflies Work"**. *Howstuffworks*. https://animals.howstuffworks.com/insects/butterfly.htm#pt2.

"Housefly - Wikipedia". 2022. *En.Wikipedia.Org*. https://en.wikipedia.org/wiki/Housefly.

"Hinny - Wikipedia". 2015. *En.Wikipedia.Org*. https://en.wikipedia.org/wiki/Hinny.

"Greenhouse Gases Are Depriving Our Oceans Of Oxygen". 2019. *UNEP*. https://www.unep.org/news-and-stories/story/greenhouse-gases-are-depriving-our-oceans-oxygen.

"Why do cats meow at Humans?" 2022. *Psychology Today*. https://www.psychologytoday.com/us/blog/all-dogs-go-heaven/201809/why-do-cats-meow-humans.

"20 Things You Didn't Know About... Mosquitoes". 2022. *Discover Magazine*. https://www.discovermagazine.com/health/20-things-you-didnt-know-about-mosquitoes.

"Where The 11 Deadliest Animals In The US Live". 2022. *Business Insider*. https://www.businessinsider.com/deadliest-animals-us-dont-include-sharks-crocodiles-dogs-cows-2019-8.

"Billions worldwide suffer from major tooth decay." 2013. *Science Daily*. https://www.sciencedaily.com/releases/2013/05/130530111145.htm

"Sex Change - Wikipedia". 2021. *En.Wikipedia.Org*. https://en.wikipedia.org/wiki/Sex_change.

"Skin And How It Functions". 2022. *Science*. https://www.nationalgeographic.com/science/article/skin-1.
"This Shrimp Packs A Punch". 2013. *Science News For Students*. https://www.sciencenewsforstudents.org/article/shrimp-packs-punch.

"How Do Giraffes Mate?". 2022. *Sciencing*. https://sciencing.com/giraffes-mate-4565765.html.

“What Animal Has The Longest Pregnancy?”. 2011. *Livescience.Com.* https://www.livescience.com/33086-what-animal-has-the-longest-pregnancy.html.

Magazine, Smithsonian, and Natasha Geiling. 2013. **“The Science Behind Honey’S Eternal Shelf Life”**. *Smithsonian Magazine.* https://www.smithsonianmag.com/science-nature/the-science-behind-honeys-eternal-shelf-life-1218690/.

Weiss, A., J. E. King, M. Inoue-Murayama, T. Matsuzawa, and A. J. Oswald. 2012. **“Evidence For A Midlife Crisis In Great Apes Consistent With The U-Shape In Human Well-Being”**. *Proceedings Of The National Academy Of Sciences* 109 (49): 19949-19952. doi:10.1073/pnas.1212592109.

“Alpaca Sales & Facts - Starline Alpacas Farmstay Resort”. 2022. *Starline Alpacas Farmstay Resort.* https://starlinealpacas.com.au/promotions/alpaca-sales-facts-2/.

“The Technology That Will Finally Stop Poachers”. 2018. *Popular Mechanics.* https://www.popularmechanics.com/science/animals/a25174825/technology-stops-poachers/.

“Tripod Stance - Wikipedia”. 2022. *En.Wikipedia.Org.* https://en.wikipedia.org/wiki/Tripod_stance.

“Australia’s Great Barrier Reef”. 2022. *NASA Jet Propulsion Laboratory (JPL).* https://www.jpl.nasa.gov/images/pia03401-australias-great-barrier-reef.

“Hummingbird Facts”. 2022. *Worldofhummingbirds.Com.* https://www.worldofhummingbirds.com/facts.php.

“These Animals Have Blue Or Yellow Blood”. 2022. Thoughtco. https://www.thoughtco.com/animals-with-blue-or-yellow-blood-3975999.

“Is It Possible To Grow Apples From Seeds?”. 2022. *The Spruce.* https://www.thespruce.com/can-you-grow-apples-from-seeds-3269511.

“IQ Tests Suggest Pigs Are Smart As Dogs, Chimps”. 2022. *Seeker*. https://www.seeker.com/iq-tests-suggest-pigs-are-smart-as-dogs-chimps-1769934406.html.

“Common Questions: What Do You Call A Group Of...?”. 2022. *Web.Archive.Org.* https://web.archive.org/web/20150320071411/http://www.npwrc.usgs.gov/about/faqs/animals/names.htm.

“Polar Bears: Species Facts, Info & More | WWF.CA”. 2022. *WWF.CA.* https://wwf.ca/species/polar-bears/.

Eplett, Layla. 2013. **"Exploring The Dromedairy: Camels And Their Milk".** *Scientific American Blog Network.* https://blogs.scientificamerican.com/guest-blog/exploring-the-dromedairy-camels-and-their-milk/.

"Bubonic Plague Still Kills Thousands". 2013. *Livescience.Com.* https://www.livescience.com/40003-plague-still-afflicts-world.html.

"Weight Of A Hummingbird". 2022. *Pets On Mom.Com.* https://animals.mom.com/weight-hummingbird-3660.html.

"Blowhole (Anatomy) - Wikipedia". 2022. *En.Wikipedia.Org.* https://en.wikipedia.org/wiki/Blowhole_(anatomy).

"Chameleon Spit Is 400 Times Thicker Than Human's". 2022. *Science.Org.* https://www.science.org/content/article/chameleon-spit-400-times-thicker-humans.

"49-Million-Year-Old Cockroach Fossil Found". 2014. *Livescience.Com.* https://www.livescience.com/42351-european-cockroach-fossils.html.

Society, National. 2015. **"Bird'S Eye View".** *National Geographic Society.* https://www.nationalgeographic.org/media/birds-eye-view-wbt/.

Dabrowski, Mark. 2022. **"The James Buchanan Brady Urological Institute | Johns Hopkins Medicine, Based In Baltimore, Md.".** *Hopkinsmedicine.Org.* https://www.hopkinsmedicine.org/brady-urology-institute/.

"Animal Facts: Turkeys". 2022. *Kidzone.Ws.* https://www.kidzone.ws/animals/turkey.htm.

"Starfish (Sea Stars) | National Geographic". 2022. *Animals.* https://www.nationalgeographic.com/animals/invertebrates/facts/starfish-1.

"Starfish (Sea Stars) | National Geographic". 2022. *Animals.* https://www.nationalgeographic.com/animals/invertebrates/facts/starfish-1.

"Why Birds Fly In A V Formation". 2022. *Science.Org.* https://www.science.org/content/article/why-birds-fly-v-formation-rev2.

"Female Glowworms With Brighter Lights Found To Attract More Mates And To Produce More Offspring". 2022. *Phys.Org.* https://phys.org/news/2015-10-female-glowworms-brighter-offspring.html.

"3-D Scans Reveal Caterpillars Turning Into Butterflies". 2022. *Science.* https://www.nationalgeographic.com/science/article/3-d-scans-caterpillars-transforming-butterflies-metamorphosis.

"Blue Whale, Facts And Photos". 2022. *Animals*. https://www.nationalgeographic.com/animals/mammals/facts/blue-whale.

"Why Do Cats Sleep So Much? 5 Facts About Sleeping Cats - Catster". 2019. *Catster*. https://www.catster.com/cat-behavior/why-do-cats-sleep-so-much-sleeping-cats-facts.

"Honey Bee Facts". 2022. *Sherbornebees.Org*. https://www.sherbornebees.org/honeybee.

HowStuffWorks, Animals, Animals, Mammals, and Mammals. 2008. **"How Long Can A Camel Go Without Water?"**. *Howstuffworks*. https://animals.howstuffworks.com/mammals/camel-go-without-water1.htm.

"Lobster Facts". 2022. *Lobstermanspage.Net*. http://www.lobstermanspage.net/lobstrs/lfacts.jsp.

Nast, Condé. 2011. **"Maned Wolf Pee Demystified"**. *Wired*. https://www.wired.com/2011/03/maned-wolf-pee-demystified/.

"Africa's deforestation twice world rate, says atlas". 2008. *Reuters*. https://www.reuters.com/article/us-africa-environment/africas-deforestation-twice-world-rate-says-atlas-idUSL1064180420080610

"The Water In You: Water And The Human Body | U.S. Geological Survey". 2022. *Usgs.Gov*. https://www.usgs.gov/special-topics/water-science-school/science/water-you-water-and-human-body.

"We May Finally Know Why Giant Beavers Didn't Survive The Ice Age". 2019. *Iflscience*. https://www.iflscience.com/plants-and-animals/we-may-finally-know-why-giant-beavers-didnt-survive-the-ice-age/.

"Bamboo - Wikipedia". 2022. *En.Wikipedia.Org*. https://en.wikipedia.org/wiki/Bamboo.

"Do Dogs Understand What They Are Seeing On Television?". 2022. *Psychology Today*. https://www.psychologytoday.com/us/blog/canine-corner/201106/do-dogs-understand-what-they-are-seeing-television.

"Surgeons find fir tree 'growing inside patient's lung". 2022. *The Telegraph*. https://www.telegraph.co.uk/news/worldnews/europe/russia/5152953/Surgeons-find-fir-tree-growing-inside-patients-lung.html.

Tsai, Michelle. 2008. **"Why Do Stingrays And Other Aquatic Creatures Leap Through The Air?"**. *Slate Magazine*. https://slate.com/news-and-politics/2008/03/why-do-stingrays-and-other-aquatic-creatures-leap-through-the-air.html.

"Short-Horned Lizard | National Geographic". 2022. *Animals.* https://www.nationalgeographic.com/animals/reptiles/facts/short-horned-lizard.

"Dust Mites: Everything You Might Not Want To Know!!!". 2022. *Ehso.Com.* https://www.ehso.com/dustmites.php.

"9 Of The Most Shocking Facts About Global Extinction - And How To Stop It". 2022. *World Economic Forum.* https://www.weforum.org/agenda/2020/11/extinction-facts-wildlife-attenborough/.

"26 Amazing Animal Facts For Kids". 2020. *Lonely Planet.* https://www.lonelyplanet.com/articles/amazing-animal-facts-for-kids.

"Upper Barataria Marsh Creation Project." 2023. *NOAA Fisheries.* https://www.fisheries.noaa.gov/southeast/habitat-conservation/upper-barataria-marsh-creation-project

"10 Snapping "Pistol Shrimp" Facts." 2023. Retrieved from https://factanimal.com/pistol-shrimp/

World Geography & Culture

Spin the globe, pick a spot, and dive in — every pinpoint on the map has a story to tell.

From Tokyo's tech wonders to the soulful music echoing through New Orleans' streets, every corner offers a different flavor of human expression.

As we navigate a world where tradition meets innovation, let's explore the places and faces that define the rich tapestry of our shared human experience.

In 2023, for the first time ever, 10 per cent of Japan's population was over 80 years old.

• • •

Previously reserved for men only, a 2023 Vatican assembly of 300 bishops from around the world gave voting rights to women.

• • •

Half of the world's population lives on a staple diet of rice.

• • •

Sheep outnumber people 6-1 in New Zealand.

A 2020 report found that birth rates in the USA have reached a three-decade low. However, while fewer women in their 20s and 30s are having children, the birth rate among 40+ women has increased.

•••

In 2022, women were appointed to high-level positions at the Vatican for the first time. The Vatican appointed three women to a committee that advises Pope Francis on candidates for Catholic church bishops.

•••

Bangladesh, facing rising sea levels, has seen innovative floating school projects that ensure education continues even in flood-prone areas.

The Statue of Liberty is made from copper. This meant that it was originally the same colour as a penny. It turned green in 1920 due to oxidation.

• • •

The main religions of Japan are Shinto and Buddhism, although religion does not play a part in the lives of most Japanese people anymore.

• • •

In 2023, American Girl (a popular collection of dolls) debuted new dolls into its historical collection: two twins named Isabel and Nicki who grew up in Seattle in the 1990s.

Times Square used to be called Longacre Square until the New York Times headquarters moved there in 1904.

• • •

Canada is south of Detroit.

• • •

The Manx language, once declared extinct, has seen a resurgence, with the Isle of Man opening its first Manx language primary school in over a century.

• • •

The world's largest ship graveyard is located in the middle of Ghana's desert; it's where ships are brought to be dismantled and scrapped.

Paris transformed its rooftops into an urban farming oasis in 2023, with the world's largest urban farm producing thousands of kilograms of produce annually right in the city.

•••

Continental plates drift at around the same pace as our fingernails grow.

•••

The largest pyramid is not in Egypt, but in Puebla, Mexico.

•••

There is a town called Boring in Oregon, which has the sister towns of Dull, Scotland and Bland, Australia.

A 2022 Gallup report found that more Americans are smoking marijuana than cigarettes for the first time in history. Around 16% of Americans reported smoking marijuana, compared to 11% smoking cigarettes. During the peak of cigarette use in the 1950s, 45% of Americans smoked.

• • •

A 2023 study found that New Zealand was one of few island nations that would be able to survive a nuclear winter as it has enough capabilities to produce enough food for its entire population.

• • •

The African continent is the only one that sits in all four hemispheres.

The African continent is experiencing a youth boom, with projections that by 2050, 1 in 4 people will be African, leading the UN to launch its first-ever Youth Office to involve young leadership.

• • •

Papua New Guinea has over 820 indigenous languages, more than in any other country.

• • •

When Queen Elizabeth II passed away at Balmoral Castle in Scotland on September 8th 2022, she was 96 years old and had reigned for 70 years, making her the second longest-reigning monarch in world history.

For the first time in modern history, Saudia Arabia essentially cancelled hajj, by barring pilgrims from visiting the holy site of Mecca during the coronavirus pandemic. Hajj is a once-in-a-lifetime pilgrimage that every Muslim tries to make if they can afford to do so.

• • •

In 2024, virtual reality heritage tours became a trend, offering immersive experiences of historical sites from the comfort of your home, from the pyramids of Egypt to the ruins of Machu Picchu.

• • •

The word 'kimono' translates to 'thing to wear'. In Japanese, 'ki' means 'wear' and 'mono' means 'thing'.

The Sargasso Sea, in the middle of the North Atlantic Ocean, has no shores. Its only borders are other seas.

• • •

Due to the International Date Line, Samoa is 24 hours ahead of American Samoa despite being only 43 miles (69 km) apart.

• • •

Europe's share of global population has declined from around 25% in 1900 to under 10% in 2000, and is projected to further decrease to around 7% by 2050.

• • •

In Taiwan, garbage trucks play music to remind people to bring out their trash, kind of like an ice cream truck.

After winning the election, Stubbs the cat was mayor of the Alaskan town of Talkeetna between 1997 and 2007.

• • •

Measured from the centre of Earth, Mount Chimborazo in Ecuador is higher than Mount Everest. Mauna Kea in Hawaii is also taller than Everest using this method.

• • •

In Vatican City, every person drinks an average of 105 bottles of wine a year — more than any other country in the world.

• • •

The Eiffel tower was originally meant to be built in Barcelona, but the citizens disapproved so it was built in Paris.

There is only one ATM in Antarctica, installed by Wells Fargo in 1998 at McMurdo Station.

• • •

One-third of seafood products in the United States are mislabelled, so you may not be eating what you think you are.

• • •

Copenhagen aims to become the world's first carbon-neutral capital by 2025, and it's well on its way with bicycles outnumbering cars!

• • •

In 2023, 27 new sites worldwide were added to the UNESCO World Heritage List, including the forest Massif of Odzala-Kokoua in Congo and the Jewish medieval historic center of Erfurt in Germany.

The average North American lives no more than 18 miles (29 km) from their mom.

• • •

There is a train between Germany and Denmark, which gets on a ship and off again at its destination. It is called Vogelfluglinie in German and Fugleflugtslinjen in Danish.

• • •

Rwanda was the first country in the world to become completely plastic-free. Residents found with single-use plastics face a jail term of up to six months.

• • •

Quito in Ecuador is said to have the world's most pleasant climate. It is nicknamed the 'Land of Eternal Spring'.

The state sport of Maryland is jousting. In fact, it was the first US state to adopt an official sport.

• • •

The last country to outlaw slavery was Mauritania, in 1981.

• • •

The Spanish national anthem has no words. The anthems of Bosnia and Herzegovina, Kosovo and San Marino also have no words.

• • •

In October 2020, Pope Francis became the first pope to indicate support for same-sex unions during an interview for the documentary 'Francesco'.

The Hawaiian alphabet has only 12 letters.

• • •

There's a museum of 'Broken Relationships' in Croatia.

• • •

The Pirahã tribe of North Western Brazil has eight consonants and three vowels in its language.

• • •

Banknotes in Australia are waterproof.

• • •

The longest river in the world is the Nile. It is 4,135 miles (6654 km) long.

Saudi Arabia is constructing The Line, a futuristic linear city designed to have no cars, streets or carbon emissions, stretching over 170 kilometers across the desert.

• • •

More than 600,000 commuters pass through New York's Penn Station every single day, making it the busiest transit hub in the Western Hemisphere.

• • •

There are spas in Austria filled only with warm beer.

• • •

On November 15th, 2022, the world surpassed 8 billion people, just 200 years after reaching a population of 1 billion in 1803.

In 1965 there were 180,000 nuns in the USA; now there are only 50,000.

• • •

In France, a Bachelor's degree will cost you €170 a year, even for international students.

• • •

There are only two countries in the world that don't offer compulsory paid maternity leave: the USA and Papua New Guinea.

• • •

The line that separates the dark and light sides of the moon is called The Lunar Terminator.

Mormons believe that the United States' constitution is a divinely inspired document.

• • •

The most common first name in the world is Muhammad (and its multiple spellings).

• • •

The capital of Liberia—Monrovia—was named after US President James Monroe.

• • •

The Democratic Republic of Congo has the highest concentration of French speakers outside of France. It is also the highest population of a country that has French as its official language—more than France itself!

Mexico has more immigrants from North America than from any other country.

• • •

Children with authoritarian parents are more likely to grow up to be Republicans.

• • •

John Quincy Adams loved to skinny dip in the Potomac River.

• • •

In Japan, it is considered rude if you tip a waiter.

In 2023, Iceland was named as the most peaceful place on Earth by the Institute for Economics and Peace for the 16th year in a row.

• • •

Approximately 6.7 per cent of the US population over 18 years of age has depression.

• • •

Around 30–50% of food produced in the world is thrown away.

• • •

There is a pizza vending machine in Italy—it can deliver custom pizzas in three minutes.

Since 2013, the number of airline passengers has more than doubled.

• • •

In Sardinia, there is a type of cheese that contains live maggots. It is called casu marzu.

• • •

The world's deepest postbox is located 10 metres underwater on the island of Susami Bay in Japan.

• • •

In Japan, there is a festival celebrating the penis. It is called the Kanamara Matsuri.

If the entire population of the world was moved to the USA, the country's population density would still be lower than that of Bangladesh.

• • •

Nauru, an island in the Pacific, is the only country in the world not to have an official capital.

• • •

The shortest verse in the Bible has just two words: "Jesus Wept" (John 11:35).

• • •

30 per cent of the Earth's uranium supply is in Australia.

Around 90 per cent of the world's population lives in the northern hemisphere.

• • •

The shortest distance between the USA and Russia is only 55 miles (88 km)—by way of the Bering Strait.

• • •

Grüner Lee—a park in Austria—is submerged in over 30 feet of water during the spring, when the snow melts.

• • •

There is a lizard in Kenya nicknamed the Spider Lizard as it looks just like Spiderman, with blue and red colourings. Its real name is the Red-headed Rock Agama.

Antarctica doesn't follow a time zone. Scientists who temporarily live there tend to follow the timezone in their home country.

• • •

Over three billion people live on less than $2.50 a day (in USD using purchasing parity power), which is roughly half of the world's population.

• • •

North Korea and Finland are only separated by one country (Russia).

• • •

A study found that video games may help lower the risk of depression.

One of the world's most expensive hotels is in Jaipur, India where the presidential suite costs USD 45,000 per night.

• • •

Before it was colonised, Africa had over 10,000 different states and groups.

• • •

King Edward Point, the capital of South Georgia and the Sandwich Islands, has the lowest population of any capital in the world—just 22.

• • •

Only nine per cent of all plastic waste ever produced has been recycled.

One-third of the entire lava erupted on Earth over the last 500 years has come from volcanoes in Iceland.

• • •

In Japan, you can get QR codes on your gravestone so that mourners can access information about the deceased on their cell phones.

• • •

In Sedona, Arizona, the golden arches at McDonald's are turquoise, to fit in with the relaxing atmosphere of the place.

• • •

The only religious buildings in Antarctica are churches.

Alaska is the northernmost, easternmost and westernmost state in the USA. This is because parts of the Alaskan Aleutian Islands cross over the 180° line of longitude, making it the easternmost state.

• • •

There is a museum in Croatia called "Froggyland", which is entirely composed of over 500 stuffed frogs posed in human positions.

• • •

The United States is home to 10 per cent of the world's active volcanoes — that's over 1,500.

• • •

The small country of Bangladesh has a larger population than Russia.

A 250-year old Banyan tree in Kolkata, India is bigger than the average Walmart.

• • •

The Mexican sombrero hat is designed very wide to be able to provide shade to the entire body.

• • •

In Italy, a man may be arrested for wearing a skirt.

• • •

Coffee beans aren't beans. They're fruit pits.

• • •

Every Alaskan citizen over the age of six months receives an oil dividend check of between around US$300-2000 per year.

In Thailand, people text 555 to each other instead of hahaha, because the number 5 is pronounced 'ha' in Thai.

• • •

In Japan, there are white strawberries with red seeds called 'The Scent of First Love'. They are very expensive to buy but are popular as wedding and birthday gifts.

• • •

Sequoia National Park in California contains the world's largest living tree—its trunk is 102 feet in circumference.

• • •

Burj Khalifa—the tallest building in the world—was built by Samsung.

The top of the Eiffel Tower leans away from the sun as the metal that is facing the sun expands upwards as it heats.

• • •

All the giant pandas in the world are owned by China. This means that any giant panda seen in a zoo around the world is actually on loan from China.

• • •

Black ice cream, made from coconut ash, became very trendy in 2016. However, New York City banned it in 2018 as it posed health risks.

Just 10 years ago, only 500 or so people in China could ski. Now, each year more than five million Chinese people visit ski resorts.

•••

In the past 15 years, global peacefulness has fallen by more than 3%, according to the 2022 Global Peace Index.

•••

Dubai imports its sand from Australia.

•••

As icebergs and glaciers melt they make a fizzing sound known as 'bergy seltzer'.

Virginia extends 95 miles further west than West Virginia.

• • •

There is an opera house on the US-Canada border where the stage is in one country and the audience in another. The Haskell Free Library and Opera House is in both Quebec and Vermont.

• • •

The University of Alaska stretches over four time zones.

• • •

In Antarctica, there is a waterfall that regularly pours out red liquid (it is oxidised salty water) and is known as Blood Falls.

Denver, Colorado currently has more marijuana dispensaries than McDonald's and Starbucks combined.

• • •

Panama is the only place in the world where you can see the sun rise on the Pacific Ocean and set on the Atlantic Ocean.

• • •

Only 10 per cent of people in the world are left-handed.

• • •

The state fish of Hawaii is the humuhumunukunukuapua'a.

The Tonle Sap River in Cambodia flows southeast to northwest half of the year, then changes direction the other half.

• • •

Around 20 per cent of Ugandans believe in witchcraft.

• • •

There are four different writing systems in Japan: Romaji, Katakana, Hiragana and Kanji.

• • •

Japan is about the same size as California but has half the population of the entire United States.

In South Korea, planes are banned from landing or taking off during the stressful annual college entrance exams, to ensure students have perfectly silent surroundings.

• • •

There are over 200 corpses on Mount Everest. Climbers use them as waypoints on their ascents. Until 2011, Russia didn't consider beer to be alcohol — it was classified as a soft drink.

• • •

Niagara Falls can freeze over if it gets cold enough.

• • •

There are around 180,000 islands in Finland.

“Live free or die” is the official state slogan of New Hampshire and is written on all license plates. Ironically, prisoners in New Hampshire make the license plates.

• • •

An ice cream shop in the USA sells black pudding and insect-flavoured ice cream.

• • •

There’s a place in Venezuela where lightning strikes almost 300 nights a year, known as Catatumbo Lightning, creating one of the world’s largest single generators of tropospheric ozone.

Mongolia is the least densely populated country in the world, offering vast landscapes with more horses than people.

• • •

Lake Baikal in Russia is the world's deepest and oldest freshwater lake, containing about 20% of the world's unfrozen freshwater reserve, and is home to more than 1,700 species of plants and animals, two-thirds of which can be found nowhere else in the world.

• • •

Of the 20 highest peaks in the USA, 17 are in Alaska, including the highest peak in North America - Denali.

Sources

World Economic Forum. (2023). **"More than 1 in 10 people in Japan are aged 80 or over. Here's how its ageing population is reshaping the country."** Available at: weforum.org/agenda/2023/09/elderly-oldest-population-world-japan/.

Povoledo, E. (2023). "Women Will Vote at a Vatican Meeting for the First Time." *The New York Times.* Available at: nytimes.com/2023/10/25/world/europe/women-vatican-synod-vote.html.

Gutoskey, E. (2023). "American Girl's New Historical Dolls Are '90s Twins." *Mental Floss.* Available at: mentalfloss.com/posts/american-girl-dolls-90s-twins.

ScienceDaily. (2023). "New Zealand one of few island nations with potential to produce enough food in a nuclear winter, researchers say." Available at: sciencedaily.com/releases/2023/02/230207191603.htm.

Wikipedia contributors. (2024). "Demographics of Europe." *Wikipedia, The Free Encyclopedia.* Available at: en.wikipedia.org/wiki/Demographics_of_Europe.

Wikipedia contributors. (2023). "Bunscoill Ghaelgagh." *Wikipedia, The Free Encyclopedia.* Available at: en.wikipedia.org/wiki/Bunscoill_Ghaelgagh.

Puckett, J. (2023). "UNESCO Just Added 27 New World Heritage Sites for 2023." *Condé Nast Traveler.* Available at: cntraveler.com/story/unesco-new-world-heritage-sites-2023.

"The CPH 2025 Climate Plan". (2024). *City of Copenhagen's official website.* Available at: urbandevelopmentcph.kk.dk/climate.

NEOM. (n.d.). "THE LINE." Available at: neom.com/en-us/regions/theline.

Beaubien, J. (2018). "Floating Schools Make Sure Kids Get To Class When The Water Rises." *NPR.* Available at: npr.org/sections/goatsandsoda/2018/09/12/646378073/floating-schools-make-sure-kids-get-to-class-when-the-water-rises.

Agrovent. (n.d.). "The largest urban farm in the world in Paris." Available at: agrovent.com/en/blog/the-largest-urban-farm-in-the-world-in-paris/.

Onix-Systems. (2024). "The Rise of Virtual Travel Experiences: Exploring the Future of Tourism." *Medium.* Available at: onix-systems.medium.com/the-rise-of-virtual-travel-experiences-exploring-the-future-of-tourism-9ffedf10e545.

United Nations Foundation. (2023). "Year in Review: The Events That Shaped Our World in 2023." Available at: unfoundation.org/blog/post/year-in-review-the-events-that-shaped-our-world-in-2023/.

"Key Facts About Rice". 2010. *The New Humanitarian.* https://www.thenewhumanitarian.org/report/91012/asia-key-facts-about-rice.

"Stats NZ Archive Website | Stats NZ". 2022. *Stats.Govt.Nz.* https://www.stats.govt.nz/about-us/stats-nz-archive-website/.

"Samoa Time Zone - Wikipedia". 2022. *En.Wikipedia.Org.* https://en.wikipedia.org/wiki/Samoa_Time_Zone.

"Times Square - Wikipedia". 2022. *En.Wikipedia.Org.* https://en.wikipedia.org/wiki/Times_Square.

"Boring, Oregon - Wikipedia". 2022. *En.Wikipedia.Org.* https://en.wikipedia.org/wiki/Boring,_Oregon.

"World Vegetarian Day." 2022. *Usatoday.Com.* https://www.usatoday.com/story/money/food/2019/09/30/world-vegetarian-day-more-meat-free-and-vegan-options-coming/3777627002/.

"WATCH: Taiwan, Beethoven And Trash". 2012. *Huffpost.* https://www.huffpost.com/entry/taiwan-garbage-trucks-music_n_1195020.

"The Highest Point Above Earth's Center Is The Peak Of Ecuador's Mount Chimborazo, Located Just One Degree South Of The Equator Where Earth's Bulge Is Greatest.". 2022. *Oceanservice.Noaa.Gov.* https://oceanservice.noaa.gov/facts/highestpoint.html.

"Bloomberg - Are You A Robot?". 2022. *Bloomberg.Com.* https://www.bloomberg.com/graphics/2017-penn-station-summer-construction-creates-commuting-hell/.

"Legal Victory over Tuition Fees". 2019. *The Local.* https://www.thelocal.fr/20191014/legal-victory-over-tuition-fees-hike-for-foreign-students-in-france/

"Which State Drinks More Wine Per Person Than Anywhere Else?". 2014. *The Independent.* https://www.independent.co.uk/news/world/europe/vatican-city-drinks-more-wine-per-person-than-anywhere-else-in-the-world-9151475.html.

"U.S. Nuns Face Shrinking Numbers And Tensions With The Vatican". 2014. *Pew Research Center.* https://www.pewresearch.org/fact-tank/2014/08/08/u-s-nuns-face-shrinking-numbers-and-tensions-with-the-vatican/.

"The World's Loneliest ATM Is In Antarctica". 2015. *Mentalfloss.Com.* https://www.mentalfloss.com/article/63741/worlds-loneliest-atm-antarctica.

"The Most Dangerous Volcanoes In The U.S., According To The Government". 2022. *Science.* https://www.nationalgeographic.com/science/article/news-most-dangerous-volcanoes-usgs-list-geology.

"Frequently Asked Questions About The Statue Of Liberty - Statue Of Liberty National Monument (U.S. National Park Service)". 2022. *Nps.Gov.* https://www.nps.gov/stli/planyourvisit/get-the-facts.htm.

"The Typical American Lives Only 18 Miles From Mom - The Boston Globe". 2022. *Bostonglobe.Com.* https://www.bostonglobe.com/news/nation/2015/12/24/the-typical-american-lives-only-miles-from-mom/iSYQglkxaqA0VUe3WWHt7K/story.html.

"Vogelfluglinie - Wikipedia". 2022. *En.Wikipedia.Org.* https://en.wikipedia.org/wiki/Vogelfluglinie.

"Continents Split Up At The Same Speed Finger Nails Grow. And That'S Fast. (Published 2016)". 2016. *Nytimes.Com.* https://www.nytimes.com/2016/07/23/science/continental-drift-tectonic-plates.html.

"The Origin Of The Eiffel Tower". 2008. *Mentalfloss.Com.* https://www.mentalfloss.com/article/18579/origin-eiffel-tower.

"Kimono - Definition, Meaning & Synonyms". 2022. *Vocabulary.Com.* https://www.vocabulary.com/dictionary/kimono.

"Slavery In Mauritania - Wikipedia". 2022. *En.Wikipedia.Org.* https://en.wikipedia.org/wiki/Slavery_in_Mauritania.

"Papua New Guinea - Wikipedia". 2020. *En.Wikipedia.Org.* https://en.wikipedia.org/wiki/Papua_New_Guinea#Languages.

“Great Pyramid Of Cholula - Wikipedia”. 2022. *En.Wikipedia.Org*. https://en.wikipedia.org/wiki/Great_Pyramid_of_Cholula.

“France To Phase Out Single-Use Plastics Starting January 1”. 2019. *France 24*. https://www.france24.com/en/20191231-france-begins-phasing-out-single-use-plastics.

“Heritage History | Our South American Neighbors By G. Southworth”. 2022. *Heritage-History.Com*. https://www.heritage-history.com/index.php?c=read&author=southworth&book=south&story=ecuador.

“Developmental Antecedents of Political Ideology: A Longitudinal Investigation From Birth to Age 18 Years”. 2012. *Sage Journal*. https://journals.sagepub.com/doi/abs/10.1177/0956797612440102.

Kühn, Simone, Fabrice Berna, Thies Lüdtke, Jürgen Gallinat, and Steffen Moritz. 2018. **“Fighting Depression: Action Video Game Play May Reduce Rumination And Increase Subjective And Objective Cognition In Depressed Patients”**. *Frontiers In Psychology 9*. doi:10.3389/fpsyg.2018.00129.

“Global Food: Waste Not, Want Not”. 2013. *Imeche.Org*. https://www.imeche.org/policy-and-press/reports/detail/global-food-waste-not-want-not.

“Why Jousting is Maryland’s Official State Sport.” 2017. *Culture Trip*. https://theculturetrip.com/north-america/usa/maryland/articles/why-jousting-is-marylands-official-state-sport/

“Marcha Real - Wikipedia”. 2021. *En.Wikipedia.Org*. https://en.wikipedia.org/wiki/Marcha_Real.

“Hawaiian Alphabet - Wikipedia”. 2022. *En.Wikipedia.Org*. https://en.wikipedia.org/wiki/Hawaiian_alphabet.

“Museum Of Broken Relationships - Wikipedia”. 2022. *En.Wikipedia.Org*. https://en.wikipedia.org/wiki/Museum_of_Broken_Relationships.

“Everett On The Pirahã Language Of Brazil - New Learning Online”. 2022. *Newlearningonline.Com*. https://newlearningonline.com/literacies/chapter-1/everett-on-the-pirahae-language-of-brazil.

“Polymer Banknote - Wikipedia”. 2022. *En.Wikipedia.Org*. https://en.wikipedia.org/wiki/Polymer_banknote.

“What’s The World’s Longest River?”. 2010. *Livescience.Com*. https://www.livescience.com/32600-what-is-the-worlds-longest-river.html.

News, Travel, All Stories, and The beer.... 2016. **"The Austrian Brewery Turned Beer Spa That Lets You Bask In Gallons Of Pints - Lonely Planet"**. *Lonely Planet*. https://www.lonelyplanet.com/articles/worlds-only-beer-spa-in-austria.

"America Is The Only Rich Country Without A Law On Paid Leave For New Parents". 2019. *The Economist*. https://www.economist.com/united-states/2019/07/18/america-is-the-only-rich-country-without-a-law-on-paid-leave-for-new-parents.

"General Astronomy/Phases Of The Moon - Wikibooks, Open Books For An Open World". 2022. *En.Wikibooks.Org*. https://en.wikibooks.org/wiki/General_Astronomy/Phases_of_the_Moon.

"The Divinely Inspired Constitution". 2022. *Churchofjesuschrist.Org*. https://www.churchofjesuschrist.org/study/ensign/1992/02/the-divinely-inspired-constitution?lang=eng.

"Muhammad (Name) - Wikipedia". 2013. *En.Wikipedia.Org*. https://en.wikipedia.org/wiki/Muhammad_(name).

"Monrovia - Wikipedia". 2022. *En.Wikipedia.Org*. https://en.wikipedia.org/wiki/Monrovia.

"The Countries That Speak The Most French (Besides France) - Frenchly". 2020. *Frenchly*. https://frenchly.us/the-countries-outside-of-france-that-speak-the-most-french/.

"Ice Cream Shop Is Serving Blood And Insect Ice Cream Pints Because Halloween". 2022. *Foodbeast.Com*. https://www.foodbeast.com/news/salt-straw-blood-insect-ice-cream/.

Dorre, Howard. 2017. **"The Skinny On John Quincy Adams's Skinny Dipping Interview"**. *Plodding Through The Presidents*. https://www.ploddingthroughthepresidents.com/2017/02/john-quincy-adams-skinny-dipping.html.

"Our Planet Is Drowning In Plastic Pollution. This World Environment Day, It's Time For A Change". 2022. *Unep.Org*. https://www.unep.org/interactive/beat-plastic-pollution/.

"Do You Tip In Japan? Japanese Tipping Etiquette | Insidejapan Tours". 2013. *Insidejapan Blog*. https://www.insidejapantours.com/blog/2013/09/22/do-you-tip-in-japan-japanese-tipping-etiquette/.

Ventura, L. (2024). World's Most Peaceful Country 2023 Global Peace Index. Available at: https://gfmag.com/data/most-peaceful-countries/

"Depression Statistics: Types, Symptoms, Treatments & More". 2022. *Healthline*. https://www.healthline.com/health/depression/facts-statistics-infographic.

Burn-Callander, Rebecca. 2009. **"24-Hour Pizza Vending Machine Let's Pizza Launches In Italy"**. *Real Business*. https://realbusiness.co.uk/24-hour-pizza-vending-machine-lets-pizza-launches-in-italy.

"Casu Martzu - Wikipedia". 2022. *En.Wikipedia.Org*. https://en.wikipedia.org/wiki/Casu_martzu.

Kawazoe, Yuika. 2013. **"Town's Undersea Mailbox Lures Divers".** *The Japan Times*. https://www.japantimes.co.jp/news/2013/07/26/national/towns-undersea-mailbox-lures-divers/.

"Kanamara Matsuri - Wikipedia". 2022. *En.Wikipedia.Org*. https://en.wikipedia.org/wiki/Kanamara_Matsuri.
Peter Kim Streatfield, Zunaid Ahsan Karar. 2008. **"Population Challenges For Bangladesh In The Coming Decades"**. *Journal Of Health, Population, And Nutrition 26* (3): 261. https://www.ncbi.nlm.nih.gov/pmc/articles/PMC2740702/.

Nast, Condé. 2013. **"Nauru: The Country Without A Capital".** *Condé Nast Traveler*. https://www.cntraveler.com/stories/2013-02-04/nauru-country-without-a-capital-maphead-ken-jennings.

"Jesus Wept - Wikipedia". 2022. *En.Wikipedia.Org*. https://en.wikipedia.org/wiki/Jesus_wept.

"Uranium Mining In Australia - Wikipedia". 2022. *En.Wikipedia.Org*. https://en.wikipedia.org/wiki/Uranium_mining_in_Australia.

"Alaska Town Elects A Cat For Mayor". 2022. *UPI*. https://web.archive.org/web/20120718101313/http:/www.upi.com/Odd_News/2012/07/15/Alaska-town-elects-a-cat-for-mayor/UPI-92141342368115/.

"Northern Hemisphere - Simple English Wikipedia, The Free Encyclopedia". 2022. *Wikipedia*. https://simple.wikipedia.org/wiki/Northern_Hemisphere.

Rastogi, Nina. 2008. **"Can You Really See Russia From Alaska?".** *Slate Magazine*. https://slate.com/news-and-politics/2008/09/can-you-really-see-russia-from-alaska.html.

“Grüner See (Styria) - Wikipedia”. 2022. *En.Wikipedia.Org*. https://en.wikipedia.org/wiki/Gr%C3%BCner_See_(Styria).

“Mpala Live! Field Guide: Red-Headed Rock Agama | Mpalalive”. 2022. *Mpalalive.Org*. https://www.mpalalive.org/field_guide/red_headed_rock_agama.

“What’s Antarctica’s Time Zone? That Depends On Who You Ask.”. 2022. *Hurtigruten.Com*. https://www.hurtigruten.com/destinations/antarctica/inspiration/antarctica-time-zone/.

“Poverty Facts And Stats”. 2013. *Globalissues.Org*. https://www.globalissues.org/article/26/poverty-facts-and-stats.

“Photos From World’s Most Expensive Hotel Rooms - E! Online”. 2014. *E! Online*. https://www.eonline.com/photos/14050/world-s-most-expensive-hotel-rooms.

“History Of Africa - Wikipedia”. 2022. *En.Wikipedia.Org*. https://en.wikipedia.org/wiki/History_of_Africa.

“Volcanism Of Iceland - Wikipedia”. 2022. *En.Wikipedia.Org*. https://en.wikipedia.org/wiki/Volcanism_of_Iceland.
Kneese, Tamara. 2014. **“Would You Get A QR Code On Your Gravestone?”**. *The Atlantic*. https://www.theatlantic.com/technology/archive/2014/05/qr-codes-for-the-dead/370901/.

“The Surprising Reason One Mcdonald’s Uses Turquoise Arches”. 2019. *Reader’s Digest*. https://www.rd.com/article/mcdonalds-turquoise-arches/.

“Religion In Antarctica - Wikipedia”. 2021. *En.Wikipedia.Org*. https://en.wikipedia.org/wiki/Religion_in_Antarctica.

“Aleutian Islands - Wikipedia”. 2023. *En.Wikipedia.Org*. https://en.wikipedia.org/wiki/Aleutian_Islands.

“Froggyland – Museum Of The Best Taxidermy In The World”. 2023. *Froggyland*. https://froggyland.net/.

“List Of Countries And Dependencies By Population - Wikipedia”. 2022. *En.Wikipedia.Org*. https://en.wikipedia.org/wiki/List_of_countries_and_dependencies_by_population.

“Sombrero - Wikipedia”. 2022. *En.Wikipedia.Org*. https://en.wikipedia.org/wiki/Sombrero.

"Unusual Italian Laws". 2022. *ITALY Magazine*. https://www.italymagazine.com/featured-story/unusual-italian-laws.

"Coffee Bean - Wikipedia". 2023. *En.Wikipedia.Org*. https://en.wikipedia.org/wiki/Coffee_bean.

"Alaska Permanent Fund - Wikipedia". 2018. *En.Wikipedia.Org*. https://en.wikipedia.org/wiki/Alaska_Permanent_Fund.

Garber, Megan. 2012. **"55555, Or, How To Laugh Online In Other Languages"**. *The Atlantic*. https://www.theatlantic.com/technology/archive/2012/12/55555-or-how-to-laugh-online-in-other-languages/266175/.

"White Strawberries: Scent of First Love." 2012. *Japan Today*. https://japan-today.com/category/features/food/white-strawberries-scent-of-first-love

"Giant Sequoias And Redwoods: The Largest And Tallest Trees". 2017. *Livescience.Com*. https://www.livescience.com/39461-sequoias-redwood-trees.html.

"Burj Khalifa - Wikipedia". 2023. *En.Wikipedia.Org*. https://en.wikipedia.org/wiki/Burj_Khalifa.

"It's Still Christmas In Armenia". 2018. *Smithsonian Magazine*. https://www.smithsonianmag.com/travel/its-still-christmas-armenia-180967689/.
"Giant Pandas Around The World - Wikipedia". 2014. *En.Wikipedia.Org*. https://en.wikipedia.org/wiki/Giant_pandas_around_the_world.

"Coconut Ash Still Trending In China Despite New York Banned". 2023. *News.Cgtn.Com*. https://news.cgtn.com/news/3d3d414d3345444f78457a6333566d54/share_p.html.

"The Chinese Skiing Boom Is In Full Swing". 2018. *Outside Online*. https://www.outsideonline.com/outdoor-adventure/snow-sports/chinese-downhill/.

News, World, and Middle News. 2022. **"Why Even Arab Nations Are Buying Sand - Times Of India"**. *The Times Of India*. https://timesofindia.indiatimes.com/world/middle-east/why-even-arab-nations-are-buying-sand/articleshow/60492513.cms.

"Bergy Seltzer | Geophysical Institute". 2022. *Gi.Alaska.Edu*. https://www.gi.alaska.edu/alaska-science-forum/bergy-seltzer.

"Virginia Extends Farther West Than West Virginia". 2004. *American Profile*. https://americanprofile.com/articles/virginia-extends-farther-west-than-west-virginia/.

“Haskell Free Library And Opera House - Wikipedia”. 2023. *En.Wikipedia.Org*. https://en.wikipedia.org/wiki/Haskell_Free_Library_and_Opera_House.

“Time Zones | Geophysical Institute”. 2023. *Gi.Alaska.Edu*. https://www.gi.alaska.edu/alaska-science-forum/time-zones.

“Blood Falls - Wikipedia”. 2022. *En.Wikipedia.Org*. https://en.wikipedia.org/wiki/Blood_Falls.

“How Many Dispensaries In Denver, Colorado? We Counted Them.”. 2018. *My 420 Tours*. https://www.my420tours.com/many-dispensaries-denver-Colorado/.

“Fun Facts — EOP”. 2022. *EOP*. https://www.embassyofpanama.org/fun-facts.

“Handedness - Wikipedia”. 2013. *En.Wikipedia.Org*. https://en.wikipedia.org/wiki/Handedness.

“Reef Triggerfish - Wikipedia”. 2023. *En.Wikipedia.Org*. https://en.wikipedia.org/wiki/Reef_triggerfish.

“Tonlé Sap - Wikipedia”. 2019. *En.Wikipedia.Org*. https://en.wikipedia.org/wiki/Tonl%C3%A9_Sap.

“Virginia Extends Farther West Than West Virginia”. 2004. *American Profile*. https://americanprofile.com/articles/virginia-extends-farther-west-than-west-virginia/.

“Haskell Free Library And Opera House - Wikipedia”. 2023. *En.Wikipedia.Org*. https://en.wikipedia.org/wiki/Haskell_Free_Library_and_Opera_House.
“Time Zones | Geophysical Institute”. 2022. *Gi.Alaska.Edu*. https://www.gi.alaska.edu/alaska-science-forum/time-zones.

“Blood Falls - Wikipedia”. 2022. *En.Wikipedia.Org*. https://en.wikipedia.org/wiki/Blood_Falls.

“How Many Dispensaries In Denver, Colorado? We Counted Them.”. 2018. *My 420 Tours*. https://www.my420tours.com/many-dispensaries-denver-colorado/.

“Fun Facts — EOP”. 2022. *EOP*. https://www.embassyofpanama.org/fun-facts.

“Handedness - Wikipedia”. 2013. *En.Wikipedia.Org*. https://en.wikipedia.org/wiki/Handedness.

"Reef Triggerfish - Wikipedia". 2022. *En.Wikipedia.Org*. https://en.wikipedia.org/wiki/Reef_triggerfish.

"Tonlé Sap - Wikipedia". 2019. *En.Wikipedia.Org*. https://en.wikipedia.org/wiki/Tonl%C3%A9_Sap.

Kennedy, Shannon, and Shannon Kennedy. 2018. **"The Ultimate Guide To Japanese Writing Systems: Learning To Read Hiragana, Katakana And Kanji | Eurolinguiste"**. *Eurolinguiste*. http://eurolinguiste.com/japanese-writing-systems/.

"Suneung: The Day Silence Falls Over South Korea". 2022. *BBC News*. https://www.bbc.com/news/world-asia-46181240.

Magazine, Smithsonian, and Rachel Nuwer. 2012. **"There Are Over 200 Bodies On Mount Everest, And They'Re Used As Landmarks"**. *Smithsonian Magazine*. https://www.smithsonianmag.com/smart-news/there-are-over-200-bodies-on-mount-everest-and-theyre-used-as-landmarks-146904416/.

"Russia Decides Beer is Alcohol, Not Food". 2011. *IB Times*. https://www.ibtimes.com/russia-decides-beer-alcohol-not-food-300825

"How Cold Is It In Canada? Niagara Falls Has Frozen Over". 2019. *Mentalfloss.Com*. https://www.mentalfloss.com/article/571434/how-cold-it-canada-niagara-falls-has-frozen-over.

"The Land Of The Hundred Thousand Lakes And Islands - Sail In Finland!". 2012. *Sail In Finland!*. https://sail-in-finland.info/2012/07/finland-the-land-of-the-hundred-thousand-lakes-and-islands/.

"Live Free Or Die - Wikipedia". 2022. *En.Wikipedia.Org*. https://en.wikipedia.org/wiki/Live_Free_or_Die.

"Here's What Happened In 2022 In 10 Striking Pictures". 2023. World Economic Forum. https://www.weforum.org/agenda/2022/12/2022-what-happened-this-year-pictures/.

Lake Baikal. (2024). https://www.britannica.com/place/Lake-Baikal

See Venezuela's Everlasting Lightning Storm. (n.d.). https://www.atlasobscura.com/videos/see-venezuela-s-everlasting-lightning-storm

Denali or Mount McKinley? (n.d.). https://www.nps.gov/dena/learn/historyculture/denali-origins.htm

Business & Politics

As the globe turns and the markets churn, 2023-24 proved to be years where the world's business and political landscapes raced ahead with the verve of a startup. The year witnessed giants of industry and new players alike adapt with agility to the post-pandemic world's changing needs.

Yet, this era of rapid progress, with AI and the digital revolution at the forefront, is juxtaposed against a backdrop of geopolitical strain not felt since the World Wars.

As businesses and governments tackle unprecedented challenges, the world watches, waits, and learns.

Let's delve into the stories of change-makers and innovators who are sculpting our modern world.

Apple Inc., as of April 2024, holds a market cap of $2.607 trillion, marking it as the second most valuable company in the world by market cap behind Microsoft. This is a slight decrease from their 2023 market cap of $2.994 trillion. In 2018, Apple was the first company to reach $1 trillion; in 2020, it reached $2 trillion.

• • •

The Secret Service was originally formed to chase counterfeiters. They started protecting the president in 1901 after president William McKinley was shot in Buffalo.

• • •

Bill Clinton met President Kennedy in the White House Rose Garden when he was a young boy in 1963.

It is estimated that 94 per cent of the world's population recognise Coke's red and white logo.

• • •

In January 2020, the UK officially left the European Union. Estimates suggest Brexit has already reduced UK real GDP by around 1% in 2020 and 2-3% in 2023, with the impact expected to gradually escalate to 5-6% of GDP by 2035. This equates to a per capita income loss of around £850 currently, potentially reaching £2,300 by 2035.

• • •

Meta, Facebook's parent company, reported its first revenue decline since its 2012 IPO in July 2022. However, in 2023 it bounced back with a 139.37% rise in value in just one year (April 2023-April 2024).

There aren't "57 varieties" of Heinz ketchup, as many people have been led to believe. Founder H.J. Heinz thought his product should have a number, and he simply liked 57.

• • •

There are no keyholes in the US presidential limousine. Only the Secret Service knows how to open it.

• • •

The man who designed the Pringles can, Fred Bauer, is buried in one—or at least some of his ashes are, at his request.

• • •

IKEA is an acronym named after the founder, the farm where he grew up and his hometown: Ingvar Kamprad Elmtaryd Agunnaryd.

The first McDonald's drive-through opened up near a military base in Arizona, because the military wasn't allowed to be seen in public in their uniforms and didn't have time to get changed to grab a quick burger or shake.

• • •

The Chinese yuan, for the first time, overtook the American dollar as the most widely used currency for cross-border payments in China in March 2023.

• • •

It takes 570 gallons (2,591 litres) to paint the exterior of the White House.

• • •

Every day, 15 per cent of the searches that occur are ones that Google has never seen before.

Around 88 percent of millionaires in the USA are self-made. Around 12 per cent inherited their wealth. Also, most of them attended college.

• • •

In 2022, Liz Truss became the shortest-serving Prime Minister in UK history after 44 days in office. In 2024 she announced she is releasing her autobiography.

• • •

The company Adobe was named after Adobe Creek, which ran behind the house of co-founder John Warnock.

• • •

One in eight Americans has at one point been employed by McDonald's.

As of early 2024, the conflict in Ukraine, which began in February 2022, continues to drive Europe's largest displacement of people since World War II, with over 6.3 million refugees seeking safety internationally and another 3.6 million displaced within the country's borders.

• • •

In 2023, the Constitution of Brazil was given an official translation into Nheengatu, one of the more widely spoken Indigenous languages in the Amazon.

• • •

According to *US Small Business*, around 20 per cent of small businesses fail in their first year.

Play-Doh was first designed as a wallpaper cleaner. In fact, it was very successful for many years. However, they later discovered that it was great for using as kids' modelling clay and it took off.

• • •

Every year, every manager at Amazon spends two days doing call-centre training—even the CEO.

• • •

Everyone that works at Ben & Jerry's headquarters can take home three pints of ice cream every single day that they work.

• • •

The name Reebok is a stylized version of the word rhebok—an African antelope.

Estonia's e-residency program, launched a few years ago, became especially popular in 2023, allowing global digital nomads to establish businesses and bank accounts remotely. By mid-2023, over 109,000 individuals had become e-residents, establishing more than 28,500 Estonian companies and generating around €37.7 million in tax revenue.

• • •

In September 2022, Yvon Chouinard, founder of Patagonia, transferred ownership of the $3 billion company to trusts and non-profits, redirecting all profits, around $100 million per year, to fight climate change.

The collapse of Silicon Valley Bank, Signature Bank, and First Republic Bank in 2023 was the most consequential US banking crisis since 2008. The combined $500 billion in assets held by these three banks exceeded the holdings of the 25 banks that failed during the 2008 financial crisis.

• • •

In 2021, Scotland became the first country to require that every school in the country should include L.G.B.T.Q. history and awareness in its curriculum.

• • •

Founded in 930, the Parliament of Iceland is the oldest acting parliament in the world.

If you have $10 in your pocket and no debt, you are wealthier than 25% of Americans.

• • •

Karl Marx was once a correspondent for the *New York Daily Tribune*.

• • •

After Donald Trump was elected in 2016, New Zealand's immigration website received 17,000 registrations of interest in one month from Americans wanting to emigrate there. They normally receive around 3,000 registrations from Americans per month.

In April 2023, Donald Trump pleaded not guilty to 34 felony charges related to hush-money payments ahead of the 2016 presidential vote. This marked him as the first former US president to be criminally prosecuted.

• • •

Up until 1910, Bayer—the company that produces health products including aspirin—sold heroin as a medicine for children suffering from coughs and colds.

• • •

Hewlett Packard, Apple and Microsoft were all started in a garage.

• • •

Steve Jobs was an executive producer on Toy Story.

The first menu item at McDonald's was a hot dog, not hamburgers.

• • •

During the war in Iraq and Afghanistan, the US Military spent over $20 billion a year on air conditioning—more than NASA's total budget.

• • •

The first five United States Presidents were never photographed.

• • •

Disney owns 80 per cent of ESPN.

• • •

President Ronald Reagan was a lifeguard during high school and saved 77 people's lives.

Kim Jong Il wrote six operas that were better than any in the history of music, according to his official biography.

• • •

The biggest selling product of all time is the Rubik's cube, followed by the iPhone. However, in terms of financial revenue, the iPhone was significantly more successful.

• • •

Mark Zuckerberg is red-green colourblind, which is why Facebook is so blue.

• • •

There are 582 million entrepreneurs worldwide.

Pennsylvania is misspelled on both the Liberty Bell and on the US Constitution. It is missing an 'n'.

• • •

At 4,400 words, the US Constitution is the shortest constitution of any major government.

• • •

If you smoke near an Apple computer, you void its warranty.

• • •

Warner Music owns the copyright to 'Happy Birthday'. Prior to 2016, the company would collect royalties when it was played in public. However, a legal case concluded in 2016 determined that the song is in the public domain, meaning it no longer requires payment for use in most situations.

Around 70 per cent of small businesses are owned and operated by a single person.

• • •

Over 84 million 'mouse ears' have been sold at Walt Disney World since it opened.

• • •

You can purchase large sheets of uncut US currency through the mail at moneyfactory.gov.

• • •

The most popular hashtag on Instagram in 2023 was #love.

• • •

Over one-third of the US population visits Walmart each week.

The World Bank states that Small and Medium Enterprises (SMEs) form the backbone of the global economy, as 90% of businesses worldwide are SMEs, generating half of the world's employment.

• • •

Bill Gates is wealthier than the GDP of 122 countries.

• • •

20 per cent of South Korea's gross domestic product comes from Samsung.

• • •

Starbucks brought in round tables so that customers would feel less alone.

Ben & Jerry’s ice cream is owned by Unilever, which also makes deodorant.

• • •

One in 10 Europeans is conceived on an Ikea bed.

• • •

Google was originally called BackRub.

• • •

Some things you say to Siri on your iPhone are stored and analysed by Apple. However, the data is anonymous.

• • •

Modern Thanksgiving was originally thought up by George Washington to give thanks to the Constitution.

The founder of FedEx once saved the company by taking its final $5,000 and gambling it in Las Vegas for a huge profit.

• • •

The YKK on zippers stands for Yoshida Kogyo Kabushiki Kaisha. The company makes around 90 per cent of all zippers in the world. Their largest factory is in Georgia and it makes over seven million zippers a day.

• • •

It is estimated that US corporations are hiding over $1.6 trillion of profits in offshore accounts.

• • •

Apple iPhone screens are mostly made by Samsung.

If it were made in the United States, the iPhone would cost $2,000.

• • •

Topeka, Kansas changed its name to 'Google' in 2010 to try and get the attention of Google executives who were selecting communities for a trial run of its new Google Fiber network.

• • •

Blasting past expectations, the global blockchain market hit a whopping $19.03 billion in 2023, with projections soaring even higher.

• • •

Every single hour, Walmart brings in over $1.8 million of profit.

Swedish automobile manufacturer, Volvo, which has a focus on safety, gave away its patent to the three-point seat belt to save lives.

• • •

Lego is the biggest producer of rubber tires in the world.

• • •

Dell Computers was started by a 19-year-old with only $1,000.

• • •

Google's old motto used to be 'Don't be evil'. They dropped it in 2015, but it is still part of their corporate code of conduct.

When he was 17, Elon Musk lived off one dollar a day for a month to see if he would be able to make it as an entrepreneur.

• • •

In 1984, the New Zealand Prime Minister called a spontaneous general election while he was drunk. He lost.

• • •

Steve Wozniak was so good at Tetris—he was the #1 player in the USA for many years—he got banned from submitting his scores to Nintendo Power magazine.

• • •

President James Madison was Princeton's first grad student.

Nintendo originally started out by producing playing cards.

• • •

The grave of Karl Marx has an entrance fee.

• • •

People in the USA get so excited about food during the Super Bowl that the sale of antacids increases by 20 per cent every year after the day of the game.

• • •

The founder of Guinness Brewery had 21 children with his one wife.

• • •

During the eight years that Bill Clinton was President, he only sent two emails.

There are more people on Facebook than there were on Earth 200 years ago.

• • •

The homewares company, IKEA, is registered as a 'not for profit', due to a claim that they are advancing architecture and interior design.

• • •

When George W. Bush was 30 years old, he was arrested for driving under the influence of alcohol. A Tupperware party starts somewhere in the world every 23 seconds.

• • •

In 2016, hackers managed to break into Mark Zuckerberg's Twitter and Pinterest accounts. They claimed his password was 'dadada'.

It costs the US Mint nearly twice as much to produce new penny and nickel coins than they are worth.

• • •

About 4.6 per cent of the population of New York City has a net worth of over $1 million. This means that one out of every 21 New Yorkers is a millionaire.

• • •

Every day around 10,000 Facebook users die. Soon, dead Facebook users will outnumber living ones.

• • •

Uber, the world's largest taxi provider, owns no vehicles of its own.

One of the chief exports of Nauru, a small island in the Western Pacific, is fossilised bird droppings (also known as phosphate).

• • •

Milton Hershey left almost his entire fortune to fund the Milton Hershey School, which was originally for orphan boys but is now open for boys and girls from over 30 states.

• • •

In 2006, the term 'to Google' was recognised by the Merriam Webster dictionary and the Oxford English Dictionary.

• • •

Google has a Klingon interface.

During the Cold War, US spies were caught by the KGB because they used high-quality American staples in their fake Soviet passports, instead of Russian ones, which would rust.

• • •

The most dangerous job in the United States is a fisherman, with 116 deaths per 10,000 workers. This is followed by logging and garbage collection.

• • •

Starbucks spends more on healthcare insurance for its employees than it does on coffee beans.

• • •

The bloodhound is the only animal whose evidence is admissible in an American court.

At the movie theatre, $30 of raw popcorn translates into $3,000 worth of sales.

• • •

Donald Trump launched his own brand of vodka, but it didn't sell very well. Maybe it's because he claims to never have sipped alcohol!

• • •

Milton Hershey, the founder of Hershey Chocolate, built the town of Hershey in Pennsylvania so that his employees could create a community where they would be self-reliant and own their own homes.

• • •

George Washington did not sign the Declaration of Independence. He was already in New York commanding troops when the Declaration was adopted.

2024 is a historic election year. More than two billion voters are set to go to the polls in 50 countries, including the US and India.

• • •

For the first time in history, Mexico's 2024 election will see two women as the leading presidential candidates.

• • •

William Henry Harrison, the shortest-serving U.S. president, gave the longest inaugural speech.

Sources

China's currency rises in cross-border trade but remains limited globally. 2023. *Goldmann Sachs.* https://www.goldmansachs.com/intelligence/pages/chinas-currency-rises-in-cross-border-trade-but-remains-limited-globally.html

STF. 2023. https://www.stf.jus.br/arquivo/cms/noticiaNoticiaStf/anexo/ConstituicaoNheengatu_WEB1.pdf.

E-Residency In Estonia Statistics [2023]. 2024. *Estonia Consulting.* https://eesticonsulting.ee/e-residency-card-in-numbers/.

Apple (AAPL) - Market capitalization. (n.d.). https://companiesmarketcap.com/apple/marketcap/.

Turits, M. (2023). Ten major events that shaped business in 2023. 2024. *BBC News.* https://www.bbc.com/worklife/article/20231219-ten-major-events-that-shaped-business-in-2023.

Dixon, H., Carbo, P. B., & Millard, S. 2024. *Revisiting the Effect of Brexit.* https://www.niesr.ac.uk/publications/revisiting-effect-brexit?type=global-economic-outlook-topical-feature.

Meta Platforms (META) Market Cap & Net Worth. (n.d.). https://stockanalysis.com/stocks/meta/market-cap/.

Ukraine emergency. (n.d.). *UNHCR.* https://www.unhcr.org/emergencies/ukraine-emergency.

Sauter, M. A., Sauter, M. A., Nelson, L. A., Uible, E., & Weigley, S. 2016) *The Best-selling Products of All Time.* https://www.foxbusiness.com/features/the-best-selling-products-of-all-time.

"Happy Birthday" song officially recognized in public domain. 2016. *CBS News.* https://www.cbsnews.com/news/happy-birthday-song-officially-recognized-in-public-domain/.

Claight Corporation - Expert Market Research. (n.d.). *Global Blockchain Technology Market Report and Forecast 2024-2032.* https://www.expertmarketresearch.com/reports/blockchain-technology-market.

2024 is a record year for #elections – here's what you need to know. 2024. *WeForum.* https://www.weforum.org/agenda/2023/12/2024-elections-around-world/.

"Chupa Chups Logo, Designed By Salvador Dali | Logo Design Love". 2013. *Logo Design Love.* https://www.logodesignlove.com/chupa-chups-logo.

Inauguration of William Henry Harrison. 2024. *Wikipedia.*https://en.wikipedia.org/wiki/Inauguration_of_William_Henry_Harrison.

"The Beginnings Of The Secret Service". 2022. *Numismatics.Org*. http://numismatics.org/the-beginnings-of-the-secret-service/.

"Bill Clinton And John F. Kennedy: The Story Behind Their 1963 Handshake". 2022. *Biography*. https://www.biography.com/news/john-f-kennedy-bill-clinton-handshake-1963.

"Who We Are | The Coca-Cola Company". 2022. *The Coca-Cola Company.* https://www.coca-colacompany.com/careers/who-we-are.

"Adobe Inc. - Wikipedia". 2022. *En.Wikipedia.Org.* https://en.wikipedia.org/wiki/Adobe_Inc.

"About IKEA – Our Heritage". 2022. *Ikea.Com.* https://www.ikea.com/us/en/this-is-ikea/about-us/our-heritage-pubde78e100.

"Fred Baur - Wikipedia". 2022. *En.Wikipedia.Org.* https://en.wikipedia.org/wiki/Fred_Baur.

"11 Things About Mcdonald's That May Surprise You". 2015. *Cbsnews.Com.* https://www.cbsnews.com/media/11-things-about-mcdonalds-that-may-surprise-you/.

"7 Customer Service Lessons From Amazon CEO Jeff Bezos". 2013. *The 360 Blog From Salesforce.* https://www.salesforce.com/blog/jeff-bezos-lessons-blog/.

"Reebok - Wikipedia". 2022. *En.Wikipedia.Org*. https://en.wikipedia.org/wiki/Reebok.

"What's The Best Part About Working At Ben & Jerry's? | Ben & Jerry's". 2022. *Benjerry.Com.* https://www.benjerry.com/flavors/3-pints-a-day.

"Althing - Wikipedia". 2022. *En.Wikipedia.Org*. https://en.wikipedia.org/wiki/Althing.

“New-York Tribune - Wikipedia”. 2022. *En.Wikipedia.Org*. https://en.wikipedia.org/wiki/New-York_Tribune.

“Bayer - Wikipedia”. 2022. *En.Wikipedia.Org*. https://en.wikipedia.org/wiki/Bayer.

“6 $25 Billion Companies That Started In A Garage”. 2014. *Inc.Com*. https://www.inc.com/drew-hendricks/6-25-billion-companies-that-started-in-a-garage.html.
“Steve Jobs”. 2022. *Pixar Wiki*. https://pixar.fandom.com/wiki/Steve_Jobs.

“Heinz® Ketchup History & Timeline | Heinz® Ketchup”. 2022. *Heinz.Com*. https://www.heinz.com/heinz-timeline.

“The White House Building | The White House”. 2022. *The White House*. https://www.whitehouse.gov/about-the-white-house/the-grounds/the-white-house/.

“McDonalds First Drive-Through”. 2022. *Azcentral.Com*. https://www.azcentral.com/story/travel/arizona/2016/08/29/mcdonalds-first-drive-through-sierra-vista-arizona/88009974/.

“More Americans Actually Moved To New Zealand Last Year”. 2022. *Fortune*. https://fortune.com/2018/02/02/us-migration-new-zealand-trump/.

HowStuffWorks, Money, Business, and Profiles. 2008. **“How Mcdonald’s Works”**. *Howstuffworks*. https://money.howstuffworks.com/mcdonalds1.htm.

“Which American President Was The First To Be Photographed?”. 2022. *HISTORY*. https://www.history.com/news/john-quincy-adams-early-photo.

“7 **Companies Owned By Disney”**. 2022. *Investopedia*. https://www.investopedia.com/articles/markets/102915/top-5-companies-owned-disney.asp.

Jennings, Richi. 2022. **“Apple Voids Applecare Warranty For Smokers!”**. *Computerworld*. https://www.computerworld.com/article/2468226/apple-voids-applecare-warranty-for-smokers-.html.

Hiskey, Daven. 2011. **“Play-Doh Was Originally Wallpaper Cleaner”**. *Today I Found Out*. http://www.todayifoundout.com/index.php/2011/11/play-doh-was-originally-wallpaper-cleaner/.

“The Strange Musical World Of Kim Jong Il | WQXR Editorial | WQXR”. 2022. *WQXR*. https://www.wqxr.org/story/176557-strange-musical-world-kim-jong-il/.

"24-7". 2022. *Usatoday.Com.* https://www.usatoday.com/story/money/business/2014/05/18/24-7-wall-st-the-best-selling-products-of-all-time/9223465/.

"Televisions Biggest Advertisers Spent Almost 10 billion in 2019." 2022. *Adweek.Com.* https://www.adweek.com/convergent-tv/televisions-biggest-advertisers-spent-almost-10-billion-in-2019/.

"Pennsylvania is spelled wrong in the constitution." 2022. *Penn Live.* https://www.pennlive.com/opinion/2015/09/us_constitution_fun_facts.html

"The Constitution Curse: And Other Facts You Didn't Know About The Constitution - One Legal". 2017. *One Legal.* https://www.onelegal.com/blog/the-constitution-curse-and-other-facts-you-didnt-know-about-the-constitution/.

"Happy Birthday To You - Wikipedia". 2022. *En.Wikipedia.Org.* https://en.wikipedia.org/wiki/Happy_Birthday_to_You.

"18 Amazing Facts About Small Businesses In America". 2022. *Business Insider.* https://www.businessinsider.com/facts-about-small-businesses-in-america-2011-8?IR=T.

"23 Crazy Facts About Disneyland". 2022. *Business Insider.* https://www.businessinsider.com/23-crazy-facts-about-disneyland-2015-7?IR=T.

"Buying, Selling, & Redeeming". 2022. *Treasury.Gov.* https://www.treasury.gov/resource-center/faqs/Currency/Pages/edu_faq_currency_sales.aspx.

"The Best Instagram Filter To Get The Most Likes, Says Study". 2018. *Yourtango.* https://www.yourtango.com/2016291359/best-instagram-filter-to-get-most-likes-says-science.

"The Grocery List: Why 140 million choose Walmart." 2016. *Walmart.* https://corporate.walmart.com/newsroom/business/20161003/the-grocery-list-why-140-million-americans-choose-walmart

"Bill Gates Net Worth Is Bigger Than GDP Of 130 Countries - Knoema.Com". 2022. *Knoema.* https://knoema.com/wqezguc/bill-gates-net-worth-is-bigger-than-gdp-of-130-countries.

Ullah, Zahra. 2022. **"How Samsung Dominates South Korea's Economy"**. *Cnnmoney.* https://money.cnn.com/2017/02/17/technology/samsung-south-korea-daily-life/index.html.

Cruz, Arlene. 2015. **"Starbucks: Round Tables At Starbucks Are They Designed To Make People Feel Less Lonely?"**. *Food World News.* https://www.foodworldnews.com/articles/15813/20150304/starbucks-round-tables-designed-make-feel-less-lonely.htm.

“List Of Unilever Brands - Wikipedia”. 2022. *En.Wikipedia.Org*. https://en.wikipedia.org/wiki/List_of_Unilever_brands.

Grandoni, Dino. 2011. **“One In Ten Europeans Were Conceived In IKEA Beds”**. *The Atlantic*. https://www.theatlantic.com/international/archive/2011/09/one-ten-europeans-were-conceived-ikea-beds/337380/.

“Google Was Originally Called Backrub”. 2022. *Gizmodo*. https://gizmodo.com/google-was-originally-called-backrub-1605435217.

“Thanksgiving”. 2022. *George Washington’s Mount Vernon*. https://www.mountvernon.org/library/digitalhistory/digital-encyclopedia/article/thanksgiving/.

“Frederick W. Smith - Wikipedia”. 2022. *En.Wikipedia.Org*. https://en.wikipedia.org/wiki/Frederick_W._Smith.

“YKK - Wikipedia”. 2022. *En.Wikipedia.Org*. https://en.wikipedia.org/wiki/YKK.

“Companies Of The United States With Untaxed Profits - Wikipedia”. 2022. *En.Wikipedia.Org*. https://en.wikipedia.org/wiki/Companies_of_the_United_States_with_untaxed_profits.

“Does Samsung Make Iphone Parts?”. 2022. *It Still Works*. https://itstillworks.com/samsung-make-iphone-parts-18028.html.

“How Much Would A ‘Made In America’ Iphone Cost? Too Much. | Mark J. Perry”. 2018. *Fee.Org*. https://fee.org/articles/a-made-in-america-iphone-would-cost-2-000-studies-show/.

“How Google Fiber Changed Kansas City”. 2022. *Wbur.Org*. https://www.wbur.org/hereandnow/2017/11/08/google-fiber-kansas-city.

“Walmart SWOT Analysis 2022 | SWOT Analysis Of Walmart”. 2019. *Business Strategy Hub*. https://bstrategyhub.com/swot-analysis-of-walmart-2019-walmart-swot-analysis/.

“A MILLION LIVES SAVED SINCE VOLVO INVENTED THE THREE-POINT SAFETY BELT”. 2022. *Media.Volvocars.Com*. https://www.media.volvocars.com/uk/en-gb/media/pressreleases/20505.

“Lego - Wikipedia”. 2022. *En.Wikipedia.Org*. https://en.wikipedia.org/wiki/Lego#Manufacturing.

"How Michael Dell turned $1000 into Billions." 2022. *CNBC*. https://www.cnbc.com/2018/02/26/how-michael-dell-turned-1000-into-billions-starting-from-his-dorm.html

"Don't Be Evil - Wikipedia". 2022. *En.Wikipedia.Org*. https://en.wikipedia.org/wiki/Don%27t_be_evil.

"Elon Musk Explains Why Living Off A Dollar A Day As A Teenager Convinced Him He Could Do Anything He Wanted With His Life". 2022. *Business Insider*. https://www.businessinsider.com/elon-musk-living-off-a-dollar-a-day-startalk-2015-3?IR=T.

"Marlboro Man - Wikipedia". 2020. *En.Wikipedia.Org*. https://en.wikipedia.org/wiki/Marlboro_Man.

"Last Meal - Wikipedia". 2022. *En.Wikipedia.Org*. https://en.wikipedia.org/wiki/Last_meal.
"1984 New Zealand General Election - Wikipedia". 2023. *En.Wikipedia.Org*. https://en.wikipedia.org/wiki/1984_New_Zealand_general_election.

"Steve Wozniak Was So Good At Tetris He Got Banned From Nintendo Power". 2022. *Gizmodo*. https://gizmodo.com/steve-wozniak-was-once-the-best-tetris-player-in-americ-1587220552.

"10 Things You May Not Know About James Madison". 2022. *HISTORY*. https://www.history.com/news/10-things-you-may-not-know-about-james-madison.

Pinsker, Joe. 2015. **"Somehow, Karl Marx's Resting Place Has An Entry Fee"**. *The Atlantic*. https://www.theatlantic.com/business/archive/2015/10/das-tomb-karl-marxs-resting-place-has-an-entry-fee/412411/.

"Super Bowl Food Shockers!". 2022. *Shape*. https://www.shape.com/healthy-eating/diet-tips/super-bowl-food-shockers-you-wont-believe.

"Arthur Guinness - Wikipedia". 2023. *En.Wikipedia.Org*. https://en.wikipedia.org/wiki/Arthur_Guinness.

LaFrance, Adrienne. 2015. **"The Truth About Bill Clinton's Emails"**. *The Atlantic*. https://www.theatlantic.com/technology/archive/2015/03/the-myth-about-bill-clintons-emails/387604/.

Roser, Max, Hannah Ritchie, and Esteban Ortiz-Ospina. 2013. **"World Population Growth"**. *Our World In Data*. https://ourworldindata.org/world-population-growth.

“Is IKEA The World’s Largest Charity?”. 2008. *Mentalfloss.Com.* https://www.mentalfloss.com/article/18575/ikea-worlds-largest-charity.

“Early Life Of George W. Bush - Wikipedia”. 2022. *En.Wikipedia.Org.* https://en.wikipedia.org/wiki/Early_life_of_George_W._Bush.

“Tupperware: How The 1950S Party Model Conquered The World”. 2023. *BBC News.* https://www.bbc.com/news/business-38880964.

“Mark Zuckerberg’s Social-Media Accounts Got Hacked, And His Password Is Terrible”. 2022. *Business Insider.* https://www.businessinsider.com/mark-zuckerberg-twitter-pinterest-accounts-hacked-linkedin-hack-facebook-passwords-2016-6?IR=T.

Sahadi, Jeanne. 2022. **“Pennies And Nickels Cost More To Make Than They’re Worth”**. *Cnnmoney*. https://money.cnn.com/2016/01/11/news/economy/u-s-coins/index.html.

“Economy Of Nauru - Wikipedia”. 2012. *En.Wikipedia.Org.* https://en.wikipedia.org/wiki/Economy_of_Nauru.
“Milton Hershey School - Wikipedia”. 2023. *En.Wikipedia.Org.* https://en.wikipedia.org/wiki/Milton_Hershey_School.

“Google (Verb) - Wikipedia”. 2023. *En.Wikipedia.Org.* https://en.wikipedia.org/wiki/Google_(verb).

“New York City is home to nearly one million millionaires”. 2019. *CNBC.* https://www.cnbc.com/2019/01/18/new-york-city-has-more-millionaires-than-any-other-city-in-the-world.html

“Techcrunch Is Part Of The Yahoo Family Of Brands”. 2022. *Techcrunch.Com.* https://techcrunch.com/2015/03/03/in-the-age-of-disintermediation-the-battle-is-all-for-the-customer-interface/.

“BBC NEWS | World | Europe | Museum Exhibits Russia’s Cold War Secrets”. 2002. *News.Bbc.Co.Uk.* http://news.bbc.co.uk/1/hi/world/europe/2065020.stm.

Pines, Michael. 2022. **“The 10 Most Dangerous Jobs In The United States”**. *Ehstoday.Com.* https://www.ehstoday.com/safety/article/21917221/the-10-most-dangerous-jobs-in-the-united-states.

“First Animal Whose Evidence Is Admissible In Court”. 2023. *Guinness World Records.* https://www.guinnessworldrecords.com/world-records/first-animal-whose-evidence-is-admissible-in-court/.

"Now Showing: Declining Sales At Theater Snack Bars". 2006. *Los Angeles Times*. https://www.latimes.com/archives/la-xpm-2006-mar-18-fi-concessions18-story.html.

"Bloomberg - On The Rocks". 2022. *Bloomberg.Com*. https://www.bloomberg.com/features/2016-trump-vodka/.

"Milton S. Hershey | Hershey, PA". 2022. *Hersheypa.Com*. https://www.hersheypa.com/about-hershey/milton-hershey.php.

"9 Things You May Not Know About The Declaration Of Independence". 2023. *HISTORY*. https://www.history.com/news/9-things-you-may-not-know-about-the-declaration-of-independence.

"21 Entrepreneur Statistics And Facts You Should Know In 2022". *2021*. Findstack. https://findstack.com/entrepreneur-statistics/.

"Elon Musk Breaks World Record For Largest Loss Of Personal Fortune In History". 2023. The Guardian. https://www.theguardian.com/technology/2023/jan/12/elon-musk-breaks-world-record-for-largest-loss-of-personal-fortune-in-history.

History

Rewind to the dawn of civilisation, over 6,000 years ago, and even further to when humans first made their mark some 200,000 years ago. From the grandeur of the Roman Empire to the brilliant minds of figures like Isaac Newton, our history is chock-full of captivating stories and ingenious breakthroughs.

As history continuously unfolds around us, we have gathered some of the most intriguing, perhaps lesser-known, tidbits that have coloured the vast mosaic of our past.

Join us on a retrospective adventure as we highlight the curious and remarkable events that have contributed to the epic saga of human history.

A full-size 3-D scan of the Titanic wreckage was revealed for the first time in May 2023, showing detailed images of both the ship and its three-mile debris field.

• • •

In August 2023, a computer science student's A.I. model extracted the ancient Greek word "porphyras" — or "purple" — from a Herculaneum scroll, one of hundreds that were buried and preserved in ash after the eruption of Mount Vesuvius in A.D. 79.

• • •

The site where Julius Caesar was stabbed opened to the public for the first time in June 2023. Rome is packed with ancient historical sites, but not all of them have been open to the public due to funding issues.

William Camden wrote the official history of Queen Elizabeth I's reign in the years after she died. His work was a foundational text for historians of the period, but Camden didn't quite record an unbiased history. New transmitting light technology used in 2023 revealed the contents of pages full of crossed-out or covered-up text, showing how Camden self-edited his version of history to curry favor with James VI and I—the king who reigned after Elizabeth I. He even included a fabricated bit about how the late queen had declared James her heir before dying.

• • •

No one is totally sure what killed composer Ludwig Van Beethoven at age 56 in 1827, but a new analysis of his hair has provided some answers. A total of around 10 feet of his hair was examined using DNA testing. Researchers found that Beethoven had a genetic predisposition to liver disease and also suffered from hepatitis B.

In June 2023, Dutch archaeologists announced that, over five years of digging in a town called Tiel, they'd discovered what they dubbed "Stonehenge of the Netherlands": a religious site created 4000 years ago that included three burial mounds, the largest of which measured 65 feet in diameter and served as a burial mound-slash-solar calendar. They also found a single glass bead in one of the graves, which is a big deal—glass wasn't made there at the time, and further analysis showed that the bead had come all the way from Mesopotamia.

• • •

During Victorian times, treadmills were used as a form of punishment for criminals.

• • •

The most successful pirate of all time was a woman. Ching Shih born in 1774 in China had 80,000 men under her command.

Abraham Lincoln's wife, Mary Todd Lincoln, was a shopaholic and racked up huge debts. She was known to use federal money and falsify documents to hide her addiction.

• • •

In the third-class accommodation on the Titanic, between 700 and 1,000 third-class passengers aboard the ship had to share just two bathtubs.

• • •

Barbie travelled into space in 1965, four years before Neil Armstrong set foot on the moon.

• • •

The Incas used a complicated system of coloured knots instead of notes to keep records.

During Queen Victoria's reign of Britain, a young boy called Edward Jones managed to break into Buckingham Palace three times—including one time where he stole the Queen's underwear. He was eventually exiled to Brazil.

• • •

The ancient Egyptians mummified not just humans but also animals such as cats, ibises, and crocodiles as part of their religious beliefs.

• • •

The word 'bug', which we often use to describe a problem with our computers, was first penned by American inventor Thomas Edison in 1878.

The number of people currently serving life in prison in the USA is more than the total prison population in the 1970s.

• • •

In Ancient Greece and Rome, doctors would use spider webs as bandages. Spider silk supposedly has antibacterial properties.

• • •

There is a nuclear bomb somewhere along the coast of the state of Georgia, which has not yet been found after being dropped there in 1958.

• • •

It is widely believed that Thomas Jefferson had at least two children with his slave Sally Hemings.

The first vacuum cleaners were horse-drawn and driven from home to home in wealthy neighbourhoods. Dust and dirt were sucked up through large gas-powered hoses that would be placed through the windows and doors of the house.

• • •

The Roman Empire was the largest contiguous empire in the history of the world. At its height, it stretched from Britain to Egypt and from Spain to Iraq.

• • •

During the Victorian times people used to say 'prunes' instead of 'cheese' before having their photos taken to ensure they looked as serious as possible. Smiling in photos was believed to only be for the uneducated.

The ancient Mayans developed one of the world's most advanced and accurate calendars. Their calendar was based on a 365-day solar year and had a 260-day sacred calendar used for religious ceremonies.

• • •

Pineapples were named after pine cones by early explorers due to their similar spiky appearance.

• • •

Prince Philip, Duke of Edinburgh, made 22,219 solo public engagements before his death on April 9, 2021.

• • •

Croissants were invented in Vienna, Austria. They didn't make it to France until the 1830s.

Ancient Egyptians used slabs of stone as pillows.

• • •

The first photograph ever taken was in 1826. It took eight hours to expose.

• • •

Pizza margherita was originally designed to represent the Italian flag: green (basil), white (mozzarella) and red (tomato). It was created for Queen Margherita of Italy in the late 1800s and it was her favourite pizza.

• • •

The Incas, who ruled over parts of South America from the 15th to the 16th century, had a complex system of government and a written language that has not been fully deciphered to this day.

The body of England's King Richard III was found underneath a parking lot in 2013.

• • •

The first rollercoasters were built in the early 19th century as a way to transport coal. However, people started offering to pay to ride on them as they were so much fun.

• • •

The term "Middle Ages" refers to the period of European history between the fall of the Roman Empire in the 5th century and the beginning of the Renaissance in the 15th century.

• • •

In 1931, China banned the book Alice in Wonderland because 'animals should not use human language'.

Cleopatra lived closer in time to the moon landing (2000 years later) than to the construction of the Great Pyramids (2500 years earlier).

• • •

Abraham Lincoln loved cats so much he once let his cat eat from the table at a formal White House dinner.

• • •

In 1913 Stalin, Hitler, Trotsky and Tito all lived in Vienna for a few months.

• • •

In Ancient Rome, it was normal for 20-40 per cent of children to be left outside to die of exposure.

Neil Armstrong and his Apollo 11 colleagues had to go through US Customs when they landed back on Earth from the moon.

• • •

In the 1950s, Soviet dictator Joseph Stalin reportedly ordered the KGB to assassinate Hollywood actor John Wayne as Stalin believed that Wayne's anti-Communist views were a threat to the Soviet Union.

• • •

During World War I, French black soldiers died at a rate three times higher than their white comrades. This was because the black soldiers were often given suicide missions.

The Great Wall of China is composed of multiple walls and fortifications constructed by various Chinese dynasties throughout history. Despite not being a single uninterrupted wall, it holds the title of longest wall in the world with a length of 13,000 miles (20,900 km).

• • •

One in every 250 US citizens worked on the Manhattan Project during the Second World War.

• • •

Engineers have said that the Leaning Tower of Pisa has straightened by 1.5 inches since 2001.

• • •

George Washington almost didn't marry Martha—he was in love with his best friend's wife, Sally Fairfax.

Canary birds were once used by miners as gas detectors.

• • •

Princeton researchers successfully turned a live cat into a functioning telephone in 1929.

• • •

Officially, the longest war in history was between the Netherlands and the Isles of Scilly. It lasted from 1651-1986. There were no casualties.

• • •

The reason why perfumes are sold at the front of department stores was originally to stop the smell of horse manure wafting into the store, back before shoppers had automobiles. It was first thought up by Harry Gordon Selfridge, founder of London's famous department store of the same name.

The word 'quarantine' comes from quarantena, meaning 40 days in old Venetian. During the Black Plague, the Venetians imposed a 40-day ban on arrivals into the city.

• • •

The phrase "Goodnight, sleep tight" originates from Shakespeare's time when mattresses were secured to bed frames by ropes. If you pulled on the ropes, the bed would tighten and become firmer to sleep on.

• • •

In 1912, a Paris orphanage held a raffle to raise money—the prizes were live babies.

• • •

England's King George I was born in Germany.

In 1800, nearly 40% of all brides were pregnant when they got married.

• • •

The very first bomb dropped by the Allies on Berlin during World War II had only one casualty —an elephant in the Berlin Zoo.

• • •

The metal rivets on your jeans aren't just for show — they were originally used to protect your jeans from tearing at weak spots. This was particularly important as they were mostly used by the working-class population.

• • •

The first law dictating minimum wage requirements in the US was instituted in 1938. The minimum hourly wage was 25 cents.

The Nazis put a $5,000 bounty on Einstein's head.

• • •

Thomas Jefferson—an avid reader—sold over 6,000 books to the government, which formed the basis of the Library of Congress.

• • •

The shortest war on record was the Anglo-Zanzibar war, which lasted a whopping 38 minutes.

• • •

Tom Hanks is a third cousin, four generations removed, of Abraham Lincoln.

• • •

The word 'music' comes from the muses, Greek goddesses of the arts.

Tiffany's, the luxury jewellery store, was founded before Italy was even a country.

• • •

Ota Benga, a 23-year-old man from Congo, was exhibited in a monkey house at the Bronx zoo, New York.

• • •

Vincent Van Gogh painted "The Starry Night" shortly after checking into a psychiatric hospital in 1889.

• • •

'Mountain Dew' was once a slang term for moonshine (homemade whiskey) in the south of the US and parts of the UK.

A remarkable find in Pompeii revealed a fresco depicting what could be a precursor to modern pizza, dating back 2,000 years. This artistic gem offers a tantalizing glimpse into ancient culinary practices

•••

The Hershey chocolate bar was used as currency overseas during World War II.

•••

In 2023, an amateur metal detectorist in the UK discovered a 16th-century pendant with connections to King Henry VIII and Katherine of Aragon.

•••

During prohibition, Al Capone made $60 million a year from selling alcohol.

The Great Pyramid of Giza has eight sides, not four.

• • •

The guillotine was still used in France right up until 1977 — the same year that the first *Star Wars* movie came out.

• • •

An intriguing discovery in 2023 revealed a sequence of four dots on a bull painted in the Lascaux Cave, France, around 21,500 years ago, representing a sophisticated “proto-writing” system predating others by at least 10,000 years

• • •

In the 1880s, cocaine was sold as a medicine to cure sore throats, headaches, colds and sleeplessness.

The swastika was originally a symbol of peace and honour. It is still used today by Buddhists, particularly in Nepal.

• • •

The Bank of America was originally called the Bank of Italy.

• • •

In 1906, a man named Joe Munch was sentenced to one minute in jail.

• • •

The oldest condoms ever found date back to the 1640s; they were made from fish and animal intestines and found in Birmingham, England.

Albert Einstein acquired citizenship for five different countries: USA, Germany, Austria, Switzerland and the Kingdom of Württemberg.

• • •

Despite popular belief, Viking helmets did not have horns on them—in fact, only one helmet from that era has been found with horns on it.

• • •

Buzz Aldrin was the first man to pee on the moon—he did so shortly after stepping off the spacecraft.

• • •

John Tyler—the 10th President of the United States—still has two grandsons that are alive.
Harvard University was founded before calculus was discovered.

In 1971, astronaut Al Shepard played golf on the moon.

• • •

During World War II, a spy named Joan Pujol Garcia received the highest honour from both the Axis and the Allies—a testament to his double agent skills.

• • •

Before he became pope, Pius II wrote a best-selling erotic book: *The Tale of Two Lovers*.

• • •

The most common sacrifice of the Mayans was a beating heart pulled from a victim's chest.

The current version of the United States flag was designed by a high school student, who initially got a B- for his design. However, the student went back to his teacher after the flag was adopted by the government, and his grade was changed to an A.

• • •

In 2008, Guatemala became the first country to recognise femicide—the murder of a woman due to her gender—as a crime.

• • •

A conman by the name of Victor Lustig managed to sell the Eiffel Tower twice. He was later caught after he fled to the USA.

In 1567, a man who was said to have the world's longest beard died after tripping over said beard while trying to escape a fire.

• • •

The 'Pinky Promise' originally meant that if anyone broke a promise they would have to cut their pinky finger off.

• • •

After the 1066 Conquest, French was the official language of England for over 300 years.

• • •

In 2007, a man by the name of Corey Taylor tried to fake his own death to get out of a phone contract. He failed.

When the first of the Egyptian pyramids were built, woolly mammoths still walked the Earth.

• • •

In the 1920s, the radioactive element Radium featured in many consumer products including toothpaste, cosmetics and even condoms.

• • •

In the 1860s, the entire central city of Chicago was raised by several feet to fix a sewage problem—and everyone just carried on their business without even noticing.

• • •

The $ sign was introduced in the late 1700s.
The wristwatch was invented in 1904.

Popcorn was discovered as an accident by the Aztec Indians.

• • •

Neil Armstrong first stepped on the moon with his left foot.

• • •

Christopher Columbus brought cacao (chocolate) beans back to Spain in 1502—his fourth voyage.

• • •

The Ancient Egyptian word for 'cat' was pronounced 'miw'.

The time difference between the Stegosaurus and Tyrannosaurus Rex is greater than the time difference between Tyrannosaurus Rex and the first humans.

• • •

Thomas Jefferson was the first US President to be inaugurated in Washington D.C.

• • •

In ancient Greece, throwing an apple at a girl was a way to propose marriage. If she caught the apple, that meant she accepted.

In ancient Athens, if a jury found you guilty of sleeping with another man's wife, the man whose wife you slept with had the right to sodomise you with a radish.

• • •

Leonardo Da Vinci could write with one hand and draw with the other at the same time.

• • •

During the Ice Age, the British would use skulls of the dead as cups.

• • •

Native Americans used pumpkin seeds for both food and medicine.

Hawaii officially became a state of the United States on August 21, 1959.

• • •

In 1836, Mexican General Santa Anna had an expensive state funeral for his amputated leg.

• • •

The last man on the moon, Gene Cernan, promised his daughter he'd write her initials on the moon. He did, and they will probably be there for tens of thousands of years.

• • •

Before the mid-19th century, dentures were often made from teeth pulled from dead soldiers.

Seatbelts became mandatory in cars in the USA on March 1, 1968.

• • •

Trained pigeons would deliver secret messages over enemy lines during wartime.

• • •

The first-ever television remote was called "Lazy Bones".

• • •

In ancient Egypt, Pharaohs would smear their servants with honey so that they would attract the flies.

The propulsion system used on subway trains was derived from the technology used in elevators.

• • •

Around 50 per cent of all US Presidents have been left-handed.

• • •

At President Andrew Jackson's funeral in 1845, his pet parrot was removed for swearing.

• • •

In early Rome, it was legal for a father to kill any member of his family.

In medieval times, animals were often put on trial and many were sent to death.

•••

In the 19th Century, there was a popular cough medicine for kids called 'Mrs Winslow's Soothing Syrup', which contained morphine.

•••

The first passengers on a hot air balloon were a sheep, a duck and a rooster.

•••

In 16th Century Canada, women would drink ground beaver testicles as a contraceptive method.

In 1492, Christopher Columbus embarked on a journey with three ships, the Nina, Pinta, and Santa Maria, in search of a new route to Asia but ended up discovering the Americas instead.

• • •

Built by William the Conqueror in 1066, The Tower of London has had a multifaceted history over its 900 years, serving as a royal palace, prison, treasury and even a zoo.

• • •

The American Revolution, which spanned from 1765 to 1783, was a pivotal moment in history where the thirteen colonies severed ties with British rule and gave birth to the United States of America.

Cuneiform, the earliest known form of writing, emerged in ancient Sumer around 3200 BCE. This writing system used a series of wedge-shaped marks that were inscribed on clay tablets.

• • •

The ancient Egyptians were true engineering marvels, constructing the first known dam, the Sadd el-Kafara, around 2925 BCE, to control the annual flooding of the Nile river.

• • •

The ancient city of Troy, made legendary by Homer's epic poem the "Iliad", has undergone destruction and reconstruction at least nine times over a period of 3,000 years. Long thought to be a myth, it was rediscovered in the late 1800s, revealing the truth behind the timeless tale.

In ancient Rome, fried canaries were considered a delicacy and it was not uncommon for people to enjoy a bowl of these fried birds as a tasty treat.

• • •

Following the Korean War, a poplar tree in the Korean Demilitarized Zone caused a deadly conflict between North Korea and the United Nations Command. The dispute over the tree-trimming escalated to a point where a full military operation, named Operation Paul Bunyan, was launched just to cut down the tree with a massive show of force.

• • •

In the 16th century, a man named Perkin Warbeck claimed to be the son of Edward IV of England and for a time convinced many European courts of his legitimacy. He led rebellions and was treated as a genuine prince before eventually being captured and executed by Henry VII of England.

The Lycurgus Cup is a Roman glass cup that changes color depending on the light direction, shifting from green to red. Created in the 4th century, it's an example of ancient nanotechnology. The effect is due to the cup's glass being impregnated with particles of gold and silver, which vary in size from 50 to 100 nanometers.

•••

Have you heard of the dancing plague of 1518? In Strasbourg, France, a woman began dancing in the street, and within a week, dozens of people joined her. By the end of the month, around 400 people were dancing uncontrollably. Many died from heart attack, stroke, or exhaustion. The cause of this phenomenon remains unexplained.

In 1919, a storage tank filled with 8 million litres (2.3 million gallons) of molasses burst in Boston, creating a molasses wave that ran through the streets at 35 mph, destroying buildings and killing 21 people. It remains one of the most bizarre disasters in American history.

• • •

In 1932, Australia faced an unexpected "enemy" – emus. A large population of emus began invading farmland in Western Australia, leading to what became known as the Emu War. Despite using machine guns, the military was unsuccessful in significantly reducing the emu population, and the birds emerged victorious.

• • •

February 1865 was the only month in recorded history that didn't have a full moon.

Sources

"NPR Cookie Consent And Choices". 2022. *Npr.Org*. https://www.npr.org/templates/story/story.php?storyId=18587608.

"Hate Working Out? Blame Evolution (Published 2021)". 2021. *Nytimes.Com*. https://www.nytimes.com/2021/01/05/books/review/exercised-daniel-lieberman.html.

"Thomas Jefferson And Sally Hemings: A Brief Account". 2021. *Monticello*. https://www.monticello.org/thomas-jefferson/jefferson-slavery/thomas-jefferson-and-sally-hemings-a-brief-account/.

"REVEALED: Mary Todd Lincoln Was A Shopaholic! (And Other First Lady Facts)". 2008. *Mentalfloss.Com*. https://www.mentalfloss.com/article/18994/revealed-mary-todd-lincoln-was-shopaholic-and-other-first-lady-facts.

"Zheng Yi Sao - Wikipedia". 2022. *En.Wikipedia.Org*. https://en.wikipedia.org/wiki/Zheng_Yi_Sao.

"The Invention Of The Vacuum Cleaner, From Horse-Drawn To High Tech | Science Museum". 2022. *Science Museum*. https://www.sciencemuseum.org.uk/objects-and-stories/everyday-wonders/invention-vacuum-cleaner.

"Why Did Ancient Egyptians Use Pillows Made Of Stone? - Ancient Pages". 2018. *Ancient Pages*. https://www.ancientpages.com/2018/06/18/why-did-ancient-egyptians-use-pillows-made-of-stone/.

"Prince Philipp, Style Icon." 2021. *New York Times*. https://www.nytimes.com/2021/04/09/fashion/prince-philip-style.html

"Milestones In Photography -- National Geographic". 2022. *Photography*. https://www.nationalgeographic.com/photography/article/milestones-photography.

Bryony Jones, CNN. 2022. **"Body Found Under Parking Lot Is King Richard III, Scientists Prove - CNN"**. *CNN*. https://edition.cnn.com/2013/02/03/world/europe/richard-iii-search-announcement/index.html.

"Raising Kids Isn'T Easy. Parenting Advice Often Makes It Harder. (Published 2019)". 2019. *Nytimes.Com.* https://www.nytimes.com/2019/01/02/books/review-act-natural-cultural-history-parenting-jennifer-traig.html.

"Alice In Wonderland Was A Banned Book But For A Weird Reason". 2016. Ripley's Believe It Or Not!. https://www.ripleys.com/weird-news/alice-wonderland-banned-book/.

"Barbie Through The Ages". 2022. *HISTORY*. https://www.history.com/news/barbie-through-the-ages.

"Spider Silk: Could 'Webicillin' Beat Infections?" 2006. *Science Daily.* https://www.sciencedaily.com/releases/2006/10/061009031730.htm

"Did You Know Margherita Pizza Was Actually Named After A Queen?". 2022. *India Today.* https://www.indiatoday.in/lifestyle/what-s-hot/story/did-you-know-margherita-pizza-was-actually-named-after-a-queen-1192775-2018-03-19.

"Fascinating Buckingham Palace Facts". 2022. *London Pass®*. https://londonpass.com/en-us/blog/buckingham-palace-facts.

"Lifers Now Exceed Entire Prison Population Of 1970 | Prison Legal News". 2022. *Prisonlegalnews.Org*. https://www.prisonlegalnews.org/news/2020/sep/1/lifers-now-exceed-entire-prison-population-1970/.

"Why Victorian Photographers Had Subjects Say 'Prunes'". 2019. *Woman's World.* https://www.womansworld.com/posts/entertainment/early-photography-strange-history-171512.

"We Thought The Incas Couldn't Write. These Knots Change Everything | New Scientist". 2022. *Newscientist.Com.* https://www.newscientist.com/article/mg23931972-600-we-thought-the-incas-couldnt-write-these-knots-change-everything/#:~:text=The%20Incas%20may%20not%20have,like%20system%20for%20recording%20numbers.

"Back From The Moon, Apollo Astronauts Had To Go Through Customs". 2019. *Space.Com.* https://www.space.com/7044-moon-apollo-astronauts-customs.html.

"More About Our Profiles". 2022. *Atomic Heritage Foundation.* https://www.atomicheritage.org/more-about-our-profiles.

Messier, Gilles. 2021. **"Why Do We Call A Software Glitch A 'Bug'?"**. *Today I Found Out.* http://www.todayifoundout.com/index.php/2021/07/why-do-we-call-a-software-glitch-a-bug/.

"Croissant - Wikipedia". 2019. *En.Wikipedia.Org*. https://en.wikipedia.org/wiki/Croissant.

"The Leaning Tower Of Pisa Has Straightened Its Posture A Bit". 2018. *Curbed*. https://archive.curbed.com/2018/11/27/18113558/leaning-tower-of-pisa-straightening.

"Domestic Canary - Wikipedia". 2022. *En.Wikipedia.Org*. https://en.wikipedia.org/wiki/Domestic_canary.

"Today I Learned: Pineapples Were Actually Named After Pine Cones". 2022. *Foodbeast.Com*. https://www.foodbeast.com/news/today-i-learned-pineapples-were-actually-named-after-pine-cones/.

14, April. 2017. **"The Cat Telephone"**. *Mudd Manuscript Library Blog*. https://blogs.princeton.edu/mudd/2017/04/the-cat-telephone/.

Museum, Presidential. 2014. **"Abraham Lincoln's Cats - Presidential Pet Museum"**. *Presidential Pet Museum*. https://www.presidentialpetmuseum.com/pets/abraham-lincoln-cats/.

"Who Started/Popularized The Department Store Perfume Gauntlet?". 2013. *History Stack Exchange*. https://history.stackexchange.com/questions/8370/who-started-popularized-the-department-store-perfume-gauntlet.

"Canvassing The Masterpieces: The Starry Night By Vincent Van Gogh - The Kazoart Contemporary Art Blog". 2021. *The Kazoart Contemporary Art Blog*. https://www.kazoart.com/blog/en/canvassing-the-masterpieces-the-starry-night-by-vincent-van-gogh/.

"The Spectacular Selfridges Department Store In London". 2018. Kasiawrites. https://kasiawrites.com/spectacular-selfridges-department-store-in-london/.

"The Spectacular Selfridges Department Store In London". 2018. *Kasiawrites*. https://kasiawrites.com/spectacular-selfridges-department-store-in-london/.

"When A Paris Foundling Hospital Held A Baby Raffle". 2022. *Time*. https://time.com/4433717/paris-baby-raffle-history/.

"George I Of Great Britain - Wikipedia". 2022. *En.Wikipedia.Org*. https://en.wikipedia.org/wiki/George_I_of_Great_Britain.

"Guess What? The First Roller Coaster In America Wasn't Actually A Roller Coaster". 2017. *Reader's Digest*. https://www.rd.com/article/first-roller-coaster/.

Oord, Christian. 2019. **"The First Bomb Dropped By The Allies On Berlin Didn't Harm Anyone But Did Hit An Elephant In Berlin Zoo!".** *WAR HISTORY ONLINE.* https://www.warhistoryonline.com/instant-articles/the-first-bomb-the-allies.html?chrome=1.

"What Those Tiny Metal Buttons On Your Jeans Are Actually For". 2016. *The Independent.* https://www.independent.co.uk/life-style/fashion/those-tiny-bits-of-metal-on-your-jeans-pockets-are-actually-really-important-a6998821.html.

"British Library". 2022. *Bl.Uk.* https://www.bl.uk/history-of-writing/articles/where-did-writing-begin.

"Albert Einstein - Wikipedia". 2022. *En.Wikipedia.Org.* https://en.wikipedia.org/wiki/Albert_Einstein.
"Jefferson's Library - Thomas Jefferson | Exhibitions - Library Of Congress". 2022. *Loc.Gov.* https://www.loc.gov/exhibits/jefferson/jefflib.html.

"Anglo-Zanzibar War - Wikipedia". 2022. *En.Wikipedia.Org.* https://en.wikipedia.org/wiki/Anglo-Zanzibar_War.

"Nancy Lincoln - Wikipedia". 2022. *En.Wikipedia.Org.* https://en.wikipedia.org/wiki/Nancy_Lincoln.

"Tiffany & Co. : When And How Was It Founded? | Theeyeofjewelry.Com". 2017. *The Eye Of Jewelry.* https://theeyeofjewelry.com/tiffany-co/tiffany-co-news/tiffany-co-when-and-how-was-it-founded/.

"Ota Benga - Wikipedia". 1916. *En.Wikipedia.Org.* https://en.wikipedia.org/wiki/Ota_Benga.

"Mountain Dew - Wikipedia". 2022. *En.Wikipedia.Org.* https://en.wikipedia.org/wiki/Mountain_Dew.

"Joey Green's Wacky Uses". 2022. *Wackyuses.Com.* https://www.wackyuses.com/weirdfacts/hershey.html.

"The Speakeasies Of The 1920S – Prohibition: An Interactive History". 2022. *Prohibition.Themobmuseum.Org.* https://prohibition.themobmuseum.org/the-history/the-prohibition-underworld/the-speakeasies-of-the-1920s/.

"Guillotine - Wikipedia". 2017. *En.Wikipedia.Org.* https://en.wikipedia.org/wiki/Guillotine.

"7 Of The Most Outrageous Medical Treatments In History". 2022. *HISTORY*. https://www.history.com/news/7-of-the-most-outrageous-medical-treatments-in-history.

"Swastika - Wikipedia". 2022. *En.Wikipedia.Org*. https://en.wikipedia.org/wiki/Swastika.

2022. *Medicinenet.Com*. https://www.medicinenet.com/script/main/art.asp?articlekey=52188.

"Albert Einstein German, Swiss And American? - Google Arts & Culture". 2022. *Google Arts & Culture*. https://artsandculture.google.com/story/4QWRAvk1sh4A8A.

"Did Vikings Really Wear Horned Helmets?". 2022. *HISTORY*. https://www.history.com/news/did-vikings-really-wear-horned-helmets.

"Buzz Aldrin - Wikipedia". 2022. *En.Wikipedia.Org*. https://en.wikipedia.org/wiki/Buzz_Aldrin.

"President John Tyler's Grandson Is Still Alive". 2018. *Mentalfloss.Com*. https://www.mentalfloss.com/article/29842/president-john-tylers-grandsons-are-still-alive.

"Harvardx". 2022. *Vpal.Harvard.Edu*. https://vpal.harvard.edu/harvard-online-harvardx.

"Today In Golf History: Alan Shepard Plays Golf On The Moon". 2022. *Golf*. https://golf.com/news/today-in-golf-history-alan-shepard-plays-golf-on-the-moon/.

"Juan Pujol García - Wikipedia". 2022. *En.Wikipedia.Org*. https://en.wikipedia.org/wiki/Juan_Pujol_Garc%C3%ADa.

"The Tale Of Two Lovers - Wikipedia". 2022. *En.Wikipedia.Org*. https://en.wikipedia.org/wiki/The_Tale_of_Two_Lovers.

"Human Sacrifice In Maya Culture - Wikipedia". 2022. *En.Wikipedia.Org*. https://en.wikipedia.org/wiki/Human_sacrifice_in_Maya_culture.

"The 50-Star American Flag Began As A High School Project—And It Only Got A B". 2017. *Reader's Digest*. https://www.rd.com/article/american-flag-high-school-project/.

"Concorde - Wikipedia". 2022. *En.Wikipedia.Org*. https://en.wikipedia.org/wiki/Concorde.

"List Of Longest Spacewalks - Wikipedia". 2022. *En.Wikipedia.Org*. https://en.wikipedia.org/wiki/List_of_longest_spacewalks.

"The FBI Would Like Everyone To Stop Shooting Lasers At Airplanes". 2012. *Smithsonian Magazine*. https://www.smithsonianmag.com/smart-news/the-fbi-would-like-everyone-to-stop-shooting-lasers-at-airplanes-65075392/.

"Femicide". 2022. *Apps.Who.Int*. https://apps.who.int/iris/bitstream/handle/10665/77421/WHO_RHR_12.38_eng.pdf?sequence=1.

"Victor Lustig - Wikipedia". 2022. *En.Wikipedia.Org*. https://en.wikipedia.org/wiki/Victor_Lustig.

"10 Bizarre Ways To Die". 2009. *Howstuffworks*. https://health.howstuffworks.com/diseases-conditions/death-dying/10-ways-to-die.htm#pt3.

"What Is The True Meaning Behind A "Pinky Promise"? | Her Campus". 2018. *Her Campus*. https://www.hercampus.com/school/tulane/what-true-meaning-behind-pinky-promise/.

"British Library". 2022. *Bl.Uk*. https://www.bl.uk/discovering-literature.

"Verizon Customer Faked Death To Escape Contract". 2007. *Wired*. https://www.wired.com/2007/08/verizon-custome/.

"Did Woolly Mammoths Still Roam Parts Of Earth When The Great Pyramids Were Built?". 2019. *Worldatlas*. https://www.worldatlas.com/articles/did-woolly-mammoths-still-roam-parts-of-earth-when-the-great-pyramids-were-built.html.

"For Years, There Was Playboy For Blind People, Then A Republican Congressman Tried To Kill It". 2017. *Medium*. https://timeline.com/playboy-braille-blind-congress-ebd9cbc6d8e0.

"Radium Historical Items Catalog". 2008. *Nrc.Gov*. https://www.nrc.gov/docs/ML1008/ML100840118.pdf.

"Raising Of Chicago - Wikipedia". 2022. *En.Wikipedia.Org*. https://en.wikipedia.org/wiki/Raising_of_Chicago.

"Where Did The Dollar Sign Come From?". 2022. *HISTORY*. https://www.history.com/news/where-did-the-dollar-sign-come-from.

"History Of Watches - Wikipedia". 2022. *En.Wikipedia.Org*. https://en.wikipedia.org/wiki/History_of_watches.

“NASA - Apollo 11 -- First Footprint On The Moon”. 2022. *Nasa.Gov.* https://www.nasa.gov/audience/forstudents/k-4/home/F_Apollo_11.html.

“About Cadbury”. 2022. *Cadbury.Com.Au.* https://www.cadbury.com.au/brand-about.

“The Stegosaurus...”. 2022. *Curiosity.com.* https://curiosity.com/topics/the-stego-saurus-was-an-ancient-relic-to-the-t-rex-curiosity/

“In Ancient Greece, Throwing An Apple At Someone Was Considered A Marriage Proposal - The Vintage News”. 2016. *The Vintage News.* https://www.thevintagenews.com/2016/09/10/ancient-greece-throwing-apple-someone-considered-marriage-proposal/?chrome=1.

“What Are Some Unusual Facts About The Ancient Greeks?”. 2022. *Quora.* https://www.quora.com/What-are-some-unusual-facts-about-the-ancient-Greeks.

“Leonardo Da Vinci ‘Could Write, Draw And Paint With Both Hands’, Experts Claim”. 2019. *The Independent.* https://www.independent.co.uk/arts-entertainment/art/news/leonardo-da-vinci-drawing-painting-write-ambidextrous-both-hands-italy-a8865611.html.

“Pumpkin”. 2022. *Wa.Kaiserpermanente.Org.* https://wa.kaiserpermanente.org/kbase/topic.jhtml?docId=hn-2151005.

“Hawaii Becomes Our 50th State”. 2022. *Americaslibrary.Gov.* https://www.americaslibrary.gov/jb/modern/jb_modern_hawaii_1.html.

“Eugene Cernan: Last Man On The Moon”. 2017. *Space.Com.* https://www.space.com/20790-eugene-cernan-astronaut-biography.html.

“The Dentures Made From The Teeth Of Dead Soldiers At Waterloo”. 2015. *BBC News.* https://www.bbc.com/news/magazine-33085031.

“Seat Belt Laws In The United States - Wikipedia”. 2022. *En.Wikipedia.Org.* https://en.wikipedia.org/wiki/Seat_belt_laws_in_the_United_States.

“War Pigeon - Wikipedia”. 2022. *En.Wikipedia.Org.* https://en.wikipedia.org/wiki/War_pigeon.

“A History Of The TV Remote Control As Told Through Its Advertising”. 2022. *Me-TV Network*. https://www.metv.com/stories/a-history-of-the-television-remote-control-as-told-through-its-advertising.

“Pharoah Pepi II – Flies And Honey | Creatinghistory.Com”. 2022. *Creatinghistory.Com*. http://www.creatinghistory.com/pharoah-pepi-ii-flies-and-honey/.

“Electromagnetic Propulsion - Wikipedia”. 2022. *En.Wikipedia.Org*. https://en.wikipedia.org/wiki/Electromagnetic_propulsion.

“How Many U.S. Presidents Were Left-Handed?”. 2015. *Govtech*. https://www.govtech.com/question-of-the-day/question-of-the-day-for-02172015.html.

“Andrew Jacksons Funeral…”. 2022. *Tennessean.Com*. https://www.tennessean.com/story/news/2015/06/07/andrew-jacksons-funeral-drew-thousands-swearing-parrot/28664493/.

“Pater Familias - Wikipedia”. 2022. *En.Wikipedia.Org*. https://en.wikipedia.org/wiki/Pater_familias.

“MRS. WINSLOW’s SOOTHING SYRUP FOR CHILDREN TEETHING (Published 1860)”. 1860. *Nytimes.Com*. https://www.nytimes.com/1860/12/01/archives/mrs-winslows-soothing-syrup-for-children-teething-letter-from-a.html.

“Fantastically Wrong: Europe’s Insane History Of Putting Animals On Trial And Executing Them”. 2014. *Wired*. https://www.wired.com/2014/09/fantastically-wrong-europes-insane-history-putting-animals-trial-executing/.

“The Fabulous Story Of The First Hot Air Balloon Flights”. 2022. *Faena*. https://www.faena.com/aleph/the-fabulous-story-of-the-first-hot-air-balloon-flights.

“What Year And Month Did Not Have A Full Moon? - Answers”. 2022. *Answers*. https://www.answers.com/Q/What_year_and_month_did_not_have_a_full_moon.

“World Contraception Day: 10 Of History’S Most Horrible Contraceptives - BBC Three”. 2018. *BBC Three*. https://www.bbc.co.uk/bbcthree/article/e671cb02-4e5e-4f52-a835-25a5dd2a5963.

“List Of United States Presidential Firsts - Wikipedia”. 2020. *En.Wikipedia.Org*. https://en.wikipedia.org/wiki/List_of_United_States_presidential_firsts.

“32 Amazing Historical Facts”. 2022. *History Hit.* https://www.historyhit.com/amazing-historical-facts/.

“Titanic in 3D”. 2023. *Magellan.* https://www.magellan.gg/titanic-in-3d/

“First word discovered in unopened Herculaneum scroll by 21yo computer science student.” (n.d.). *Scroll Prize.* https://scrollprize.org/firstletters

Magazine, S. 2023. **“You Can Now Visit the Site Where Julius Caesar Was Stabbed.”** https://www.smithsonianmag.com/smart-news/julius-caesar-murder-rome-180982409/

“Hidden for 400 Years, Censored Pages Reveal New Insights Into Elizabeth I’s Reign” 2023. *Magazine, S.* https://www.smithsonianmag.com/smart-news/hidden-for-400-years-censored-pages-reveal-new-insights-on-elizabeth-is-reign-180982554/

“DNA Analysis of Beethoven’s Hair Reveals New Clues About His Death.” 2023. *Rossen, J.* https://www.mentalfloss.com/posts/beethoven-hair-dna-analysis-cause-of-death

“Dutch unveil 4,000-year-old ’Stonehenge’-like discovery.” 2023. *X, S.* https://phys.org/news/2023-06-dutch-unveil-year-old-stonehenge-like-discovery.html

“117 Fascinating Finds Revealed in 2023.” 2023. *Smithsonian.* https://www.smithsonianmag.com/history/117-fascinating-finds-revealed-in-2023-180983491/

“Here Are 12 of the Most Astounding Archaeological Discoveries of 2023.” 2023. *Artnet News.* https://news.artnet.com/art-world/best-archaeological-discoveries-2023-2410707

“Emu War.” 2024. *Wikipedia.* https://en.wikipedia.org/wiki/Emu_War

“Great Molasses Flood.” 2024. *Britannica.* https://www.britannica.com/topic/Great-Molasses-Flood

“What Was the Dancing Plague of 1518?” (n.d.). *History.com.* https://www.history.com/news/what-was-the-dancing-plague-of-1518

"Discover the Lycurgus Cup ". (n.d.). *Google Arts & Culture.* https://artsandculture.google.com/story/discover-the-lycurgus-cup/mwWBqnUNwgBpLQ?hl=en

"Perkin Warbeck." 2024. *Britannica.* https://www.britannica.com/biography/Perkin-Warbeck-English-pretender

"Korea Tree Incident: Operation Paul Bunyan: Clements National Security Papers Project." (n.d.). *Clements Papers.* Retrieved from https://ns.clementspapers.org/briefing-books/korea-tree-incident

Music & Entertainment

As we groove into 2024, the world of music and entertainment continues to be our universal language and the ultimate escape.

This is the era where blockbusters are born in the flash of a TikTok clip, and platinum records are as likely to be recorded in a teenager's bedroom as they are in a major label's studio.

Virtual concerts now bring the front row to your living room, and surprise album drops are the norm.

Even amid the reverberations of 2023's industry-shaking writer's strikes, the beat went on. Social media was awash with a Barbie-pink hue, and whether you're a Swiftie or not, it was hard not to get swept away with the global sensation that was her Eras tour.

So, let's hit play on this journey through the most tweet-worthy, streamable, and danceable moments that define our past and present.

In 2023, for the first time, streaming video-on-demand services' viewership in the United States surpassed cable and broadcast TV.

• • •

The Best Actor race at the 2023 Oscars was made up entirely of first-time nominees, which hadn't happened since 1935.

• • •

In 2023, an average of 103,500 tracks were uploaded to streaming services every day. Surprisingly, 43% of these tracks had 10 or fewer streams throughout the year, highlighting a massive gap between the most and least listened to songs.

Vinyl records continued their resurgence, with artists selling 6.8 million vinyl records directly to fans in 2023, a 40% increase from the previous year. Vinyl albums continued to outsell CDs for the third consecutive year, reaching the highest level since the first half of 2013.

• • •

Taylor Swift's "1989 (Taylor's Version)" vinyl sold 1.01 million copies in the U.S. alone upon its release.

• • •

In 2023, regional Mexican music saw a significant rise in the U.S., with a 60% increase in streams across audio and video platforms.

Spanish-language music represented 8.1% of U.S. music streams, showing a growing diversity in the American musical landscape.

• • •

In 2023, London's West End became the first major European city to celebrate Ramadan by illuminating with 30,000 festive lights.

• • •

Jimin, a member of the K-pop group BTS, made history by becoming the first South Korean solo artist to top Billboard's Hot 100 chart with his single "Like Crazy" in April 2023.

Greta Gerwig's "Barbie," featuring Margot Robbie and Ryan Gosling, made a remarkable debut, earning $162 million in the U.S. during its opening weekend. The film's global earnings surpassed $1.4 billion, making Gerwig the highest-grossing female director in history.

• • •

A Taylor Swift concert in Seattle reportedly caused seismic activity equivalent to a 2.3-magnitude earthquake, attributed to the movement of approximately 70,000 attendees.

• • •

Nintendo announced the closure of its 3DS and Wii U e-shops in March 2023, ceasing new software downloads for these consoles, although internet access remains available.

Beyoncé and Jay-Z fans had the unique opportunity to purchase items from the couple's rented home, including a bidet listed for $2400 on eBay.

• • •

"Sesame Street" introduced its first Filipino American muppet, TJ, in 2023. This character is a 4-year-old who enjoys basketball, dancing, and learning Tagalog with his grandmother, reflecting the show's ongoing commitment to diversity and representation.

• • •

In Japan, AI pop stars have become a cultural phenomenon, performing concerts attended by thousands and showcasing the country's innovative approach to entertainment and technology. Alfred Hitchcock was afraid of the dark, eggs and solitude.

During WWI, Walt Disney tried to join the military at 16 but was rejected. He later joined the Red Cross by faking his age, and was sent to France as an ambulance driver, where he helped with post-war operations after the armistice in 1918.

• • •

Al Gore and Tommy Lee Jones were freshman roommates at Harvard University.

• • •

The original voice of the narrator of *Thomas the Tank Engine* was Ringo Starr, from The Beatles.

• • •

Every episode of *Friends* mentions the word 'friends' at least once.

In the 2021 movie, *Dune*, the water-preserving suits worn by the actors were designed to be toilet-friendly—well, for the men anyway. Actress Sharon Duncan-Brewster said the ladies did not get such a privilege.

• • •

In 2002, Jared Hess, a BYU film student, created the short film “Peluca.” He later turned it into the feature-length film “Napoleon Dynamite,” which was shot in Idaho for $400,000 and grossed over $44 million at the box office after its release in 2004.

• • •

In 2000, Blink-182’s music video for “All the Small Things” parodied boy bands of the time by filming on a California beach and mimicking their choreography. Incidentally, in 2011, One Direction filmed their own music video for "What Makes You Beautiful" on the same beach, paralleling the video though it is uncertain if they drew inspiration from Blink-182.

• • •

Dolly Parton used her nails as an instrument in the song "9 to 5," achieving a typewriter-like sound by tapping her acrylic nails together. She revealed this in a 2019 appearance on *The Tonight Show with Jimmy Fallon*, and there's even a credit for the nails' performance on the album.

• • •

"Last Christmas" by Wham! is a Christmas classic but only reached No.1 on the UK charts 36 years after its release in 1984, blocked from the top spot by Band Aid's "Do They Know It's Christmas," which also featured George Michael.

The iconic shower scene in Alfred Hitchcock's "Psycho" was filmed with chocolate syrup instead of blood to avoid censorship issues.

• • •

The famous line "Here's looking at you, kid" from Casablanca was not in the original script, but was improvised by Humphrey Bogart during filming.

• • •

Stanley Kubrick's "2001: A Space Odyssey" was originally going to have a voice-over narration, but Kubrick ultimately decided to leave the film mostly dialogue-free.

• • •

The famous "I'll be back" line from "The Terminator" was improvised by Arnold Schwarzenegger while filming the scene.

The sound of the T-Rex in the film *Jurassic Park* was created by combining the sounds of various animals, including a baby elephant, a walrus, and a tiger.

• • •

Woody Allen's real name is Allen Stewart Konigsberg.

• • •

The first band to perform live on all seven continents was Metallica. They played in Antarctica in 2013.

• • •

What do Miss Piggy and Yoda have in common? They were both voiced by the same person—puppeteer Frank Oz. He was also the voice of the Cookie Monster, Bert and Grover in *Sesame Street*.

The original title of the movie *The Lion King* was 'King of the Jungle' until producers realised that lions don't live in the jungle.

• • •

Around 94 per cent of television-owning Americans watched the moon landing in 1969.

• • •

Actor Jake Gyllenhaal's first driving lesson was from Paul Newman, who was a close family friend.

• • •

George Clooney slept in a friend's closet for a year when he first moved to LA.

Cookie Monster from *Sesame Street*'s real name is Sid.

• • •

Your heartbeat changes depending on the music you're listening to.

• • •

In the music industry, for every $1,000 of music sold, the average musician gets $23.40.

• • •

The Beatles officially broke up at Disney World.

The deepest underground concert was held in 2020.

• • •

The Shaft Bottom Boys performed a set at 6,213 feet below sea level in the Vale's Creighton Mine in Sudbury, Ontario.

• • •

Charlize Theron was "discovered" when an agent witnessed her throwing a fit at a bank teller who wouldn't cash her check.

• • •

In 2020, Kurt Cobain's guitar, which he played while recording the album *"MTV Unplugged in New York"* sold for $6 million at auction, making it the most expensive guitar ever sold.

Russell Brand was legally entitled to take $20 million from Katy Perry's fortune when they divorced but refused to take any.

• • •

The movie *Paranormal Activity* cost $15000 to make and grossed $210 million.

• • •

To thank Robin Williams for his work on *Aladdin*, and to settle a dispute they had between them, Disney sent him a late Pablo Picasso painting worth $1 million.

• • •

Harry Styles has two extra nipples.

Photographer Dario Calmese became the first black photographer to shoot the cover of famed Vanity Fair magazine. He shot actor Viola Davis for the July-August 2020 issue.

• • •

Ryan Gosling was cast as Noah in *The Notebook* because the director wanted someone "not handsome."

• • •

Brad Pitt's first job was as a chicken mascot at a fast-food restaurant.

• • •

Elton John is Eminem's A.A. sponsor.

Lisa Kudrow was originally cast as Roz in *Frasier* but was fired before it aired.

• • •

Jon Cryer, from *Two and a Half Men*, was offered the role of Chandler in *Friends* but turned it down.

• • •

Sarah Jessica Parker was the only actor in *Sex and the City* to have a no-nudity clause in her contract.

• • •

Cynthia Nixon is a natural blonde, so had to dye her hair red for her role in *Sex and the City*.

The *Desperate Housewives* set was previously used in Kelly Rowland and Nelly's video for "*Dilemma*".

• • •

Emilia Clarke, who plays Daenerys in *Game of Thrones*, voiced Dr Zoidberg's girlfriend in the final episodes of Futurama.

• • •

Selma Blair and Katie Holmes were in the running to play Buffy in *Buffy the Vampire Slaye*r.

• • •

Shakira was rejected from her school's choir because they thought she sounded like a goat.

Americans cast more votes in the voting of Taylor Hicks in American Idol than in the 1984 presidential election of Ronald Reagan.

• • •

Madonna suffers from brontophobia—a fear of thunderstorms.

• • •

Daniel Craig used to sleep on park benches when he was a struggling actor.

• • •

Oprah's birth name was 'Orpah', named after the sister of Ruth in the Bible. She changed it because so many people got it wrong.

Alfred Hitchcock's *Psycho* (1960) was the first American film ever to show a flushing toilet.

• • •

Taylor Swift's first job was to knock praying mantises off Christmas trees at the farm her parents owned.

• • •

Bender from Futurama was named after John Bender from *The Breakfast Club*.

• • •

In *Saving Private Ryan* all of the main cast were given basic military training except Matt Damon, in the hope that the cast would build resentment towards him necessary for the role.

Darth Vader only has 12 minutes of screen time in the original *Star Wars*.

• • •

The movie *Saw* was filmed in 18 days.

• • •

Pierce Brosnan was contractually forbidden from wearing a full tuxedo in any non-James Bond movie from 1995-2002.

• • •

The charcoal drawing of Kate Winslet in *Titanic* was drawn by James Cameron.

Many scenes in the movie *28 Days Later* were filmed on a Canon XL-1 DV camera using mini-DV tapes instead of 35mm film.

• • •

Daniel Radcliffe's stunt double was paralysed during the last Harry Potter film, so he set up a fundraiser to pay for him to go to college.

• • •

E.T. and *Poltergeist* were originally meant to be one movie.

• • •

Beyonce has trained herself to be able to sing while running a mile, which helps prepare her for her high-energy concerts.

Sean Connery wore a wig in every James Bond film. Elton John's real name is Reginald Dwight.

• • •

Barbie in *Toy Story 2* and *3* is voiced by Jodi Benson, best known for her role as Ariel in *The Little Mermaid*.

• • •

Actor John Hurt has died in more than 40 movies—a world record.

• • •

Beethoven began losing his hearing at the age of 28, so he cut off the legs of his piano so he could compose music by feeling the vibrations of the piano on the floor.

It cost more to make the movie *Titanic* than it did to build the original ship.

• • •

During one episode of the cartoon *Pokemon,* flashing graphics sent 618 Japanese children to the hospital with seizures and nausea.

• • •

Django Unchained was the first time in 16 years that Leonardo DiCaprio didn't get the top billing.

• • •

The sound of the velociraptors mating in *Jurassic Par*k is actually the sound of tortoises mating.

• • •

Star Wars was originally prefixed with 'The'.

The chills you get when you listen to music is mostly caused by the brain releasing dopamine—a feel-good chemical—while anticipating the peak moment of a song.

• • •

Actor Tim Allen (*Home Improvement,* Buzz Lightyear) spent two years in prison for trafficking cocaine.

• • •

Ricky Martin's real name is Enrique Martín Morales.

• • •

The Partridge Family actor, Brian Forster, is the great-great-great-grandson of Charles Dickens.

Playing music regularly can alter your brain structure.

• • •

James Franco worked at McDonald's after dropping out of UCLA. He would practice his foreign accents on customers.

• • •

Robert De Niro dropped out of high school to head straight to acting school.

• • •

Jack Nicholson grew up thinking his grandmother was his mum and his mum his sister. He was born to his 'sister' when she was 17. He didn't find out until he was 37 and both of them had passed away.

Paul McCartney never learned to read music.

• • •

Johannes Brahms got his start playing the piano in brothels.

• • •

The first CD to be pressed in the USA was Bruce Springsteen's *Born in the USA*.

• • •

The first cell phone was invented in 1924.

• • •

During the filming of *Wolf of Wall Street*, Jonah Hill snorted so much fake cocaine that he got bronchitis.

Kate Bosworth has one blue eye and one hazel eye. The condition is known as heterochromia.

• • •

Rowan Atkinson (aka Mr Bean) is a qualified Electrical Engineer.

• • •

During the filming of *X-Men*, Hugh Jackman went through approximately 700 claws for his role as Wolverine.

• • •

On average, Americans spend over 11 hours a day consuming digital media.

Jean-Claude Van Damme was once homeless and lived on the streets of Los Angeles.

• • •

The most-searched-for tutorial video on Youtube is 'how to kiss'.

• • •

In December 2021, Kim Taehyung 'V', from the Korean boyband BTS, became the fastest person to reach one million followers on Instagram, in just 43 minutes.

• • •

Ashton Kutcher has a condition called syndactyly, meaning his toes are webbed together.

Robert De Niro saw the Twin Towers collapse from the window of his New York home.

• • •

Before her death in 2021, Betty White was older than sliced bread. That's right, sliced bread was introduced in 1928 and Betty White was born in 1922.

• • •

Jason Statham was on the British National Swimming squad for 12 years before becoming a Hollywood actor.

• • •

Brian May, the lead guitarist of Queen, has a PhD in Astrophysics.

A study has found that Snapchat provokes more jealousy in relationships than Facebook.

• • •

Supermodel Karolina Kurkova has no belly button. It was removed during an operation when she was younger.

• • •

Mortimer Mouse was the original name for Mickey Mouse. Walt Disney's wife was the one who convinced him to change it.

• • •

Seth Macfarlane, creator of *Family Guy*, had a ticket booked for one of the ill-fated 9/11 flights but missed it.

In the first *Dumb & Dumber* movie, Jeff Daniels made just $50,000, while Jim Carrey was paid $7 million.

• • •

While filming *I am Legend,* Will Smith got so attached to his German Shepherd co-star, that he asked if he could keep her, but the owner refused.

• • •

There's a hotline in Germany called 'Schimpf-Los' which means 'swear away'. People can call the number to let off steam after a stressful day.

• • •

Paul McCartney is the only musician to top the music charts as a solo artist, in a duo, trio, quartet and quintet.

Olympic gold medallist, George Foreman, has five sons who are all called George.

• • •

Facebook will accept three versions of your password: as it is; case inverted (in case you left caps lock on); and the password with the first letter capitalized (for mobile devices, which often automatically start with a capital).

• • •

Long before he became an actor/comedian, Ricky Gervais was part of the 80s glam-pop duo Seona Dancing.

• • •

Elvis Presley was born blonde but thought that black hair was cooler. He would sometimes even touch his colour up with shoe polish.

In 1967, the Beatles almost bought an island off the coast of Athens, Greece with plans to build a utopian community.

•••

Brad Pitt tore his Achilles tendon while playing the role of Achilles in the movie *Troy*.

•••

Popeye's four nephews are called Pipeye, Peepeye, Pupeye and Poopeye.

•••

In 2013, Mark Zuckerberg spent 30 million dollars buying four houses that surround his own home to ensure he had privacy.

The voice of Chris in *Family Guy* is based on Buffalo Bill from *Silence of the Lambs*.

• • •

Paul McCartney was once kicked out of Germany for lighting a condom on fire.

• • •

The Grammy Awards updated their rules in 2023 to restrict AI-generated songs, clarifying that songs fully generated by AI would not be considered for awards, though those with "meaningful" human contributions could still qualify.

Michael Jackson's music video for "Thriller" was the first music video to be added to the National Film Registry by the Library of Congress for being "culturally, historically, or aesthetically significant."

• • •

On average, TikTok enthusiasts are not just casually scrolling; they're dedicating about 95 minutes daily to the app, with the average user opening the app 19 times a day.

• • •

Salvador Dali designed the Chupa Chups logo in 1969. He also insisted that it was placed on the top of the wrapper so everyone could see it.

Sources

"20 Things That Happened for the First Time in 2023." 2023. *Tisak, T.*. https://www.nytimes.com/2023/12/05/special-series/20-things-that-happened-for-the-first-time-in-2023.html

"Jimin's "Like Crazy" Debuts Atop Billboard Hot 100, First Solo No. 1 for a BTS Member." 2023. *Trust, G.* https://www.billboard.com/music/chart-beat/jimin-like-crazy-debuts-number-one-first-bts-solo-hot-100-1235297097/

""Barbie" is about to become America's highest-grossing movie of 2023 | CNN Business." 2023. *Valinsky, J.* https://edition.cnn.com/2023/08/23/media/barbie-super-mario-bros-box-office/index.html

""Swift Quake": Taylor Swift Fans Shake Ground During Seattle Concert." 2023. *Che, C.* https://www.nytimes.com/2023/07/28/arts/music/taylor-swift-earthquake-seattle-.html

"When Does 3DS And Wii U Online Shut Down? Nintendo eShop & Online Play Closure Guide." 2023. *Reynolds, O.* https://www.nintendolife.com/guides/when-does-3ds-and-wii-u-online-shut-down-nintendo-eshop-and-online-play-closure-guide

"Jay-Z & Beyoncé's Household Items Go Up For Sale On eBay." 2023. *TMZ.* https://www.tmz.com/2023/06/19/jay-z-beyonce-house-items-sale-ebay/

"Sesame Street" Just Debuted Its First-Ever Filipino American Muppet. 2023. *Gutoskey, E.* https://www.mentalfloss.com/posts/sesame-street-tj-first-filipino-american-muppet

"Top 10 Famous Virtual Idols in Japan [2023 Updated]." 2023. *Phuc, D.* https://animost.com/industry-updates/10-famous-virtual-idols-in-japan/

"Media and entertainment industry; media and entertainment industry outlook." 2023. *Deloitte.* https://www.deloitte.com/global/en/Industries/tmt/perspectives/media-and-entertainment-industry-outlook.html

"Oscars 2023 trivia: the firsts, facts, and potential records worth knowing ahead of this year's show." 2023. *Yahoo.* https://guce.yahoo.com/copyConsent?sessionId=3_cc-session_95d03280-a6b8-4723-a7a5-4c852c2e5139&lang=es-ES.

“Numbers that Will Define the Music Industry 2024”. 2024. *Fast Company.* https://www.fastcompany.com/91009342/fix-numbers-that-will-define-the-music-industry-2024

“RIAA Mid-Year 2023 Revenue Report.” 2023. *Connelly, R.* https://www.riaa.com/riaa-mid-year-2023-revenue-report/

“How Prince Philip Navigated The Most Challenging Of Corporate Dress Codes”. 2021. *Nytimes.Com.* https://www.nytimes.com/2021/04/09/fashion/prince-philip-style.html.

“Art & Media”. 2022. *Treehugger*. https://www.treehugger.com/art-and-media-4846013.

“Woody Allen - Wikipedia”. 2022. *En.Wikipedia.Org.* https://en.wikipedia.org/wiki/Woody_Allen.

“15 Amazing Things We Never Knew About Jake Gyllenhaal”. 2017. *Thethings*. https://www.thethings.com/15-amazing-things-we-never-knew-about-jake-gyllenhaal/.

“George Clooney News & Biography - Empire”. 1961. *Empireonline.Com.* https://www.empireonline.com/people/george-clooney/7/.

Peeples, Lynne. 2009. **“Heart Beat: Music May Help Keep Your Cardiovascular System In Tune”**. *Scientific American.* https://www.scientificamerican.com/article/music-therapy-heart-cardiovascular/.

“Why The Lion King Had To Drop Its Original Title”. 2016. *Digital Spy.* https://www.digitalspy.com/movies/a805689/the-lion-king-alternate-title/.

“RIAA Accounting: Why Even Major Label Musicians Rarely Make Money From Album Sales”. 2022. *Techdirt..* https://www.techdirt.com/articles/20100712/23482610186.shtml.

“Dune Ending: Sharon Duncan-Brewster On Final Shot And Liet Kynes – The Hollywood Reporter”. 2022. *Hollywoodreporter.Com.* https://www.hollywoodreporter.com/movies/movie-features/dune-sharon-duncan-brewster-on-kynes-key-scenes-1235037410/.

“Frank Oz - Wikipedia”. 2022. *En.Wikipedia.Org.* https://en.wikipedia.org/wiki/Frank_Oz.

“Cookie Monster’S First Name Is Sid, And Other Icon’S “Real” Names”. 2014. *Smithsonian Magazine*. https://www.smithsonianmag.com/smart-news/cookie-monsters-first-name-sid-and-other-icons-real-names-180950099/.

"The Fountain In The Friends Opening Credits Has Been Lying To You This WHOLE Time". 2016. *Cosmopolitan*. https://www.cosmopolitan.com/uk/entertainment/news/a29836/friends-facts-33-things-you-never-knew/.

"The Apollo 11 Mission Was Also A Global Media Sensation (Published 2019)". 2019. Nytimes.Com. https://www.nytimes.com/2019/07/15/business/media/apollo-11-television-media.html.

"Breaking Breakfast News: Froot Loops Are All The Same Flavor". 2022. *Time*. https://time.com/1477/breaking-breakfast-news-froot-loops-are-all-the-same-flavor/.

"Ringo Starr". 2022. *Thomas The Tank Engine Wikia*. https://ttte.fandom.com/wiki/Ringo_Starr.

"Sam Panopoulos - Wikipedia". 2022. *En.Wikipedia.Org*. https://en.wikipedia.org/wiki/Sam_Panopoulos.

"Metallica Become First Band To Play On Seven Continents With Antarctica Gig". 2013. *Guinness World Records*. https://www.guinnessworldrecords.com/news/2013/12/metallica-become-first-band-to-play-on-seven-continents-with-antarctica-gig-53609.

Laney, Karen, 2011. **"John Lennon Officially Ended The Beatles At Disney World"**. *Ultimate Classic Rock*. https://ultimateclassicrock.com/john-lennon-ended-beatles-at-disney/.

"Charlize Theron - Imdb". 2022 **Imdb**. https://www.imdb.com/name/nm0000234/bio.

"Russell Brand says no to Katy Perry's $44 million fortune in 'amicable' divorce" 2020. *News.com.au*. https://www.news.com.au/entertainment/celebrity-life/russell-brand-says-no-to-katy-perrys-fortune-in-amicable-divorce/news-story/4f7a7300fb53743e88677f4d2b6f0b3b

"Paranormal Activity - Wikipedia". 2022. *En.Wikipedia.Org*. https://en.wikipedia.org/wiki/Paranormal_Activity.

"Robin Williams Once Got So Upset With Disney That The Company Sent Him A $1 Million Picasso Peace Offering". 2022. *Business Insider*. https://www.businessinsider.com/robin-williams-disney-feud-picasso-gift-2014-11?IR=T.

"Harry Styles Has Four Nipples, And That's More Common Than You Think". 2017. *Allure*. https://www.allure.com/story/harry-styles-confirms-he-has-four-nipples.

“Behind-The-Scenes Secrets That Every Fan Of ‘The Notebook’ Needs To Know”. 2018. *Woman’s Day*. https://www.womansday.com/life/entertainment/g24674622/notebook-movie-facts/.

“Behind-The-Scenes Secrets That Every Fan Of ‘The Notebook’ Needs To Know”. 2018. *Woman’s Day*. https://www.womansday.com/life/entertainment/g24674622/notebook-movie-facts/.

“Why Lisa Kudrow Was Fired From Frasier”. 2019. *Screenrant*. https://screenrant.com/lisa-kudrow-fired-from-frasier-reasons/.

“These Celebrities Almost Played Your Favourite Friends”. 2022. *Celebrity.Nine.Com.Au*. https://celebrity.nine.com.au/tv/these-stars-almost-played-your-favourite-friends/157786d4-dbfb-4be6-9fa9-b0bf74c396c3.

“Sarah Jessica Parker Explains Why She Has A No-Nudity Contract Clause”. 2022. *Instyle*. https://www.instyle.com/news/sarah-jessica-parker-no-nudity-contract-clause.

“12 Famous Redheads That Are Actually Blonde”. 2022. *Insider*. https://www.insider.com/red-hair-celebrities-that-are-naturally-blonde.

“How Elton John Helped Other Celebrities Struggling With Addiction”. 2019. *Page Six*. https://pagesix.com/2019/10/16/how-elton-john-helped-other-celebrities-struggling-with-addiction/.

“Dilemma (Song) - Wikipedia”. 2022. *En.Wikipedia.Org*. https://en.wikipedia.org/wiki/Dilemma_(song).

“Stench And Stenchibility - Wikipedia”. 2022. *En.Wikipedia.Org*. https://en.wikipedia.org/wiki/Stench_and_Stenchibility.

“Buffy The Vampire Slayer - Wikipedia”. 2022. *En.Wikipedia.Org*. https://en.wikipedia.org/wiki/Buffy_the_Vampire_Slayer.

“Shakira’s Teacher Told Her She Had A Bad Voice And Banned Her From The School Choir”. 2022. *Business Insider*. https://www.businessinsider.com/shakira-banned-from-school-choir-2016-3?IR=T.

“Madonna”. 2024. *Zimbio*. https://www.zimbio.com/Famous+Fears+and+Phobias/articles/vq_H6VMOzuq/Madonna.

“15 Rich And Famous People Who Were Once Homeless”. 2022. *Business Insider*. https://www.businessinsider.in/careers/15-rich-and-famous-people-who-were-once-homeless/slidelist/40128079.cms.

"Oprah Winfrey - Wikipedia". 2022. *En.Wikipedia.Org*. https://en.wikipedia.org/wiki/Oprah_Winfrey.

"14 Facts About Alfred Hitchcock's Psycho". 2015. *Mentalfloss.Com*. https://www.mentalfloss.com/article/68248/14-crazy-facts-about-psycho.

Dukes, Billy, 2012. **"10 Things You Didn'T Know About Taylor Swift"**. *Taste Of Country*. https://tasteofcountry.com/10-things-you-didnt-know-about-taylor-swift-7/.

"The Surprising Origins Of TV Character Names". 2014. *Mentalfloss.Com*. https://www.mentalfloss.com/article/57016/surprising-origins-tv-character-names.

"Saving Private Ryan - Wikipedia". 2022. *En.Wikipedia.Org*. https://en.wikipedia.org/wiki/Saving_Private_Ryan.

White, Mark, 2014. **"10 Classic Film Characters Who Didn't Have As Much Screen-Time As You Thought"**. *Whatculture.Com*. https://whatculture.com/film/10-classic-film-characters-didnt-much-screen-time-thought.

"Saw (2004 Film) - Wikipedia". 2022. *En.Wikipedia.Org*. https://en.wikipedia.org/wiki/Saw_(2004_film).

"28 Days Later - Wikipedia". 2022. *En.Wikipedia.Org*. https://en.wikipedia.org/wiki/28_Days_Later.

Smith, Louie. 2014. **"Harry Potter Stuntman David Holmes Speaks Of Moment He Was Left Paralysed In Horror Film Accident"**. *Mirror*. https://www.mirror.co.uk/news/real-life-stories/harry-potter-stuntman-david-holmes-3279214.

"Beyoncé Belted Her Entire Album While Running — Providing Further Proof That She Is A Queen". 2022. *Insider*. https://www.insider.com/beyonce-training-secret-singing-while-running-2017-11.

"007 Sean Connery, Wore A Hairpiece In Every Bond Movie He Was In - The Vintage News". 2017. *The Vintage News*. https://www.thevintagenews.com/2017/04/29/sean-connery-wore-a-hairpiece-in-every-of-his-bond-performances/?chrome=1.

"Elton John - Wikipedia". 2024. *En.Wikipedia.Org*. https://en.wikipedia.org/wiki/Elton_John.

"Jodi Benson - Wikipedia". 2024. *En.Wikipedia.Org*. https://en.wikipedia.org/wiki/Jodi_Benson.

"Ludwig Van Beethoven". 2024. *Lifeprint.Com.* https://www.lifeprint.com/asl101/topics/beethoven02.htm.

"Titanic (1997) - Imdb". 2022. *Imdb.* https://www.imdb.com/title/tt0120338/trivia.

"Flashing Japan Cartoon Makes Children Sick". 1997. *Los Angeles Times.* https://www.latimes.com/archives/la-xpm-1997-dec-17-mn-64975-story.html.

"Django Unchained (2012) - Imdb". 2022. *Imdb.* https://www.imdb.com/title/tt1853728/trivia.

Crew, Bec. 2022. **"The Raptor Noises In Jurassic Park Are Mating Tortoises"**. *Sciencealert.* https://www.sciencealert.com/the-raptor-noises-in-jurassic-park-are-mating-tortoises.

"Star Wars (Film) - Wikipedia". 2022. *En.Wikipedia.Org.* https://en.wikipedia.org/wiki/Star_Wars_(film).

"Musical thrills, why they give us chills". 2011. *Science Daily.* https://www.sciencedaily.com/releases/2011/01/110112111117.htm

"Tim Allen - Wikipedia". 2024. *En.Wikipedia.Org.* https://en.wikipedia.org/wiki/Tim_Allen.
"Ricky Martin - Wikipedia". 2024. *En.Wikipedia.Org.* https://en.wikipedia.org/wiki/Ricky_Martin.

"Brian Forster - Wikipedia". 2024. *En.Wikipedia.Org.* https://en.wikipedia.org/wiki/Brian_Forster.

"Learning With Music Can Change Brain Structure". 2017. *Neuroscience News.* https://neurosciencenews.com/music-learning-brain-structure-7037/.

"James Franco Discusses Dropping Out Of UCLA And Working At Mcdonald's - Variety". 2022. *Variety.Com.* https://variety.com/2017/tv/news/james-franco-dustin-hoffman-actors-on-actors-1202628665/.

"Robert De Niro - Wikipedia". 2024. *En.Wikipedia.Org.* https://en.wikipedia.org/wiki/Robert_De_Niro.

"Jack Nicholson's Mother". 2024. *Snopes.Com.* https://www.snopes.com/fact-check/you-dont-know-jack/.

"Paul Mccartney Admits He And The Beatles Can't Read Or Write Music - National | Globalnews.Ca". 2022. *Global News.* https://globalnews.ca/news/4503916/paul-mccartney-cant-read-music/.

"Bruce Springsteen's "Born In The U.S.A." Becomes The First Music CD Pressed In The U.S.A. : History Of Information". 1984. *Historyofinformation.Com.* https://www.historyofinformation.com/detail.php?entryid=3541.

"Jonah Hill Ended Up In Hospital After Snorting Too Much Fake Cocaine For Wolf Of Wall Street". 2019. *The Independent.* https://www.independent.co.uk/news/people/jonah-hill-fake-cocaine-wolf-of-wall-street-a7200886.html.

"Interesting Facts About Heterochromia". 2022. *All About Vision.* https://www.allaboutvision.com/conditions/heterochromia.htm.

"Rowan Atkinson - Wikipedia". 2022. *En.Wikipedia.Org.* https://en.wikipedia.org/wiki/Rowan_Atkinson.

"5 Facts About Hugh Jackman's Role As Wolverine To Get You Ready For LOGAN". 2017. *Playbuzz.* https://www.playbuzz.com/johnnybosshart10/5-facts-about-hugh-jackmans-role-as-wolverine-to-get-you-ready-for-logan.

"Time Flies: U.S. Adults Now Spend Nearly Half A Day Interacting With Media". 2018. *Nielsen.Com.* https://www.nielsen.com/us/en/insights/article/2018/time-flies-us-adults-now-spend-nearly-half-a-day-interacting-with-media/.

"Jean-Claude Van Damme - Wikipedia". 2022. *En.Wikipedia.Org.* https://en.wikipedia.org/wiki/Jean-Claude_Van_Damme.

"Youtube Viewers Really Want To Learn How To Kiss". 2015. *Fast Company.* https://www.fastcompany.com/3046271/youtube-viewers-really-want-to-learn-how-to-kiss.

"Webbed Toes - Wikipedia". 2008. *En.Wikipedia.Org.* https://en.wikipedia.org/wiki/Webbed_toes.

"Robert De Niro, Martin Scorsese Reflect On The Birth Of The Tribeca Film Festival – The Hollywood Reporter". 2022. *Hollywoodreporter.Com.* https://www.hollywoodreporter.com/movies/movie-news/tribeca-de-niro-martin-scorsese-181208/.

"Betty White Is Older Than Sliced Bread.". 2022. *Just A Pinch Recipes*. https://www.justapinch.com/groups/discuss/205417/betty-white-is-older-than-sliced-bread.

"Jason Statham - Wikipedia". 2020. *En.Wikipedia.Org*. https://en.wikipedia.org/wiki/Jason_Statham.

"Matthew Perry Is Missing The Tip Of His Finger And An Eagle-Eyed 'Friends' Viewer Finally Noticed". 2019. *Ruin My Week*. https://ruinmyweek.com/entertainment/matthew-perry-finger-friends/.

"Brian May - Wikipedia". 2022. *En.Wikipedia.Org*. https://en.wikipedia.org/wiki/Brian_May.

Hennessy, See. 2015. **"Snapchat Is Worse For Your Relationship Than Facebook"**. *Thejournal.Ie*. https://www.thejournal.ie/snapchat-facebook-jealousy-2018616-Mar2015/.

"Karolina Kurkova's Missing Bellybutton Explained (PHOTOS)". 2008. *Huffpost UK*. https://www.huffpost.com/entry/karolina-kurkovas-missing_n_145684.

"Mickey Mouse - Wikipedia". 2017. *En.Wikipedia.Org*. https://en.wikipedia.org/wiki/Mickey_Mouse.

"Seth Macfarlane, The Brains Behind 'Family Guy', Missed One Of The Doomed 9/11 Flights". 2016. *Ladbible.Com*. https://www.ladbible.com/more/interesting-creator-of-family-guy-missed-one-of-the-doomed-911-flights-20160527.

"Yahoo Is Part Of The Yahoo Family Of Brands". 2022. *Yahoo.Com*. https://www.yahoo.com/entertainment/farrelly-brothers-reveal-jim-carrey-made-7-million-for-102378340427.html

"Will Smith Falls In Love With 'Legend' Co-Star". 2007. *TODAY.Com*. https://www.today.com/popculture/will-smith-falls-love-legend-co-star-wbna22264942.

"Pipes Of Peace (Song) - Wikipedia". 2022. *En.Wikipedia.Org*. https://en.wikipedia.org/wiki/Pipes_of_Peace_(song).

"George Foreman - Wikipedia". 2022. *En.Wikipedia.Org.* https://en.wikipedia.org/wiki/George_Foreman.

"Seona Dancing - Wikipedia". 2020. *En.Wikipedia.Org.* https://en.wikipedia.org/wiki/Seona_Dancing.

"Old Photo Proves Elvis Presley Was Actually Blonde". 2019. *Country Music Nation.* https://countrymusicnation.com/old-photo-proves-elvis-presley-was-actually-blonde.

"26 July 1967: The Beatles Visit A Greek Island They Intended To Purchase". 2022. *Beatlesbible.Com.* https://www.beatlesbible.com/1967/07/26/beatles-visit-greek-island/.

"Brad Pitt Goes To Extremes In 'Troy'". 2004. *TODAY.Com.* https://www.today.com/popculture/brad-pitt-goes-extremes-troy-wbna4953083.

"Pipeye, Peepeye, Poopeye And Pupeye". 2022. *Popeye The Sailorpedia.* https://popeye.fandom.com/wiki/Pipeye,_Peepeye,_Poopeye_and_Pupeye.

"Mark Zuckerberg Just Spent More Than $30 Million Buying 4 Neighboring Houses For Privacy". 2022. *Business Insider*. https://www.businessinsider.com/mark-zuckerberg-buys-4-homes-for-privacy-2013-10.

"Stew-Roids - Wikipedia". 2022. *En.Wikipedia.Org.* https://en.wikipedia.org/wiki/Stew-Roids.

"29 November 1960: Paul Mccartney And Pete Best Are Arrested In Hamburg". 2022. *Beatlesbible.Com.* https://www.beatlesbible.com/1960/11/29/paul-mccartney-pete-best-arrested-hamburg/.

"TikTok by the Numbers (2024): Stats, Demographics & Fun Facts." 2024. https://www.omnicoreagency.com/tiktok-statistics/

Art & Literature

In our fast-paced digital era, the vibrant worlds of literature and art remain our steadfast companions. While technology races ahead, these timeless forms of expression continue to hold a cherished place in our lives, bridging the past with the present.

From the provocative works of Banksy to the imaginative tales of J. K. Rowling, art and literature provoke, inspire, and connect us all.

In this chapter, we celebrate the stories behind the stories of art in all its forms. Let's dive into some of the little-known facts from some of our favourite authors and artists.

The Oxford Dictionary added lots of new entries in 2023, including ‘groomzilla’, ‘comfort wear’ and ‘spider-sense’.

• • •

‘Dreamt’ is the only word in the English language that ends in the letters ‘mt’.

• • •

Freelancers originally referred to self-employed, sword-wielding mercenaries: literally “free lancers.”

• • •

Dr Seuss wrote *Green Eggs and Ham* as a bet against his publisher who said he couldn’t write a book with only 50 words.

There was an outbreak of head lice among the cast of *Harry Potter and the Chamber of Secrets.*

• • •

In 2023, the digital lending from libraries and schools surged to 662 million checkouts, a significant 19% increase from the previous year

• • •

The least frequently used letters in the English alphabet are J, Q, X, and Z.

• • •

Despite a global trend towards digital, physical book sales saw significant growth in in 2023 in Italy, the Netherlands, and Spain, with double-digit increases compared to pre-pandemic figures.

Emily Brontë once had to put out her brother Branwell when he set fire to his bedclothes.

• • •

Written language was invented independently by the Egyptians, Sumerians, Chinese, and Mayans.

• • •

Before settling on his pen name of Mark Twain, Samuel Langhorne Clemens signed his writings with the pseudonym 'Josh'.

• • •

When you use ? and ! together, it's called an interrobang.

People who read are two and a half times less likely to be diagnosed with Alzheimer's.

• • •

In 2023, the UK experienced a bumper year for books, with print sales up two percent, reaching €2 billion, and audio downloads increased by eight percent.

• • •

The word 'strengths' is the longest word in the English language with only one vowel.

• • •

More than 750 million adults around the world cannot read or write.

The record for most people balancing books on their heads at the same place and time is 998 in Sydney, Australia, in 2012.

• • •

Reading fiction books has been proven to improve empathy.

• • •

The first novel written on a typewriter was Mark Twain's *Adventures Of Tom Sawyer.*

• • •

Shakespeare was also an actor and performed in many of his plays.

74% of Americans said they read at least one book per year.

• • •

William Shakespeare is credited as having contributed over 2,000 new words to the existing English dictionary we all use today.

• • •

J.K. Rowling is the only person on the Forbes rich list whose source of wealth is 'selling novels'.

• • •

Harper Lee initially threw her book *To Kill a Mockingbird* out of her window into the snow. It hasn't been out of print since it was published over 70 years ago.

Before the book *Peter Pan* was written, the name Wendy was considered to be a man's name. Later, it became a popular girl's name.

• • •

The world's most expensive book ever purchased was bought by Bill Gates for $30.8 million. It was Codex Leicester by Leonardo Da Vinci.

• • •

Dr Seuss included the word 'contraceptive' in a draft of his children's book *Hop on Pop* to make sure his publisher was paying attention.

• • •

The earliest recorded use of 'wicked' to mean 'cool, good' is from F. Scott Fitzgerald's first novel, *This Side of Paradise.*

As a schoolboy in England, Roald Dahl was a taste-tester for Cadbury's chocolate.

• • •

Sting wrote the song *Every Breath You Take* at the same desk which Ian Fleming used to write his James Bond novels. It was at the 'Fleming Villa' in Jamaica.

• • •

In 1871, Mark Twain invented one of the first bra clasps.

• • •

People in India are the world's biggest readers, spending an average of 10.7 hours a week reading.

J. K. Rowling came up with the names for the houses at Hogwarts in Harry Potter while she was on a plane. She jotted the names down on a sick bag.

• • •

The best-selling fiction book of all time is *A Tale of Two Cities* by Charles Dickens.

• • •

Charles Dickens believed in ghosts and he belonged to The Ghost Club.

• • •

The original manuscript of John Steinbeck's *Of Mice and Men* was eaten by his dog, Toby.

One of William Shakespeare's relatives on his mother's side, William Arden, was arrested for plotting against Queen Elizabeth I, imprisoned in the Tower of London and then executed.

• • •

To *Kill a Mockingbird* was Harper Lee's only novel until *Go Set a Watchman*, which was an early draft of *To Kill a Mockingbird*, was published in 2015.

• • •

The original version of Roald Dahl's *Charlie and the Chocolate Factory* had several racist references; it has since been edited.

Pride and Prejudice was originally called *First Impressions.*

• • •

Poet Samuel Taylor Coleridge joined the army under the name Silas Tomkyn Cumberbatch.

• • •

In May 2022, “Shot Sage Blue Marilyn,” a silk screen of Marilyn Monroe’s face by Andy Warhol, sold for $195 million at a Christie’s auction, breaking the previous record set in 2017 by a Jean-Michel Basquiat painting as the most expensive American artwork sold at auction.

The most translated author in history is Agatha Christie, whose books have been translated into over 100 languages.

• • •

The world's longest novel, based on word count, is *Artamène ou le Grand Cyrus*, written by Madeleine de Scudéry and published in 1649-1653. It has over 4 million words and over 10 volumes.

• • •

The Harry Potter series is the fastest-selling book series of all time, with the final book, Harry Potter and the Deathly Hallows, selling over 11 million copies in the first 24 hours.

The oldest known love story in the world is the *Epic of Gilgamesh*, a Mesopotamian poem written around 2100 BCE. It tells the story of the love between the hero Gilgamesh and the goddess-turned-mortal Enkidu.

• • •

The world's smallest book is *Tiny Book of Tiny Stories*, which measures only 0.9x0.9mm and contains only 24 pages. It was created by Brazilian artist Eduardo Sanson and was entered into the Guinness World Records in 2010.

• • •

During World War II, British author Roald Dahl worked for the British Government's Psychological Warfare Division, where he was tasked with creating propaganda to be dropped over enemy territory. Dahl also wrote short stories to boost the morale of the troops.

The famous novel *Moby Dick* by Herman Melville was initially intended to be a short story, but it ended up being over 200,000 words long.

• • •

The first science fiction book was written by a woman, Mary Shelley's *Frankenstein* in 1818.

• • •

"War and Peace" by Leo Tolstoy is considered to be one of the longest novels ever written. It has over 587,287 words and around 1,225 pages.

• • •

The Adventures of Huckleberry Finn by Mark Twain is one of the most banned books in American history.

The Catcher in the Rye by J.D. Salinger is considered one of the most influential books of the 20th century, and it is said that it has been referenced in over 25,000 pieces of literature, film, and music.

• • •

The Harry Potter series was rejected by 12 publishers before finally getting accepted.

• • •

The best-selling fiction book of all time is *Don Quixote* by Miguel de Cervantes, which has sold over 500 million copies worldwide.

The first novel ever written was *The Tale of Genji* by Japanese noblewoman Murasaki Shikibu in the 11th century. It is a classic work of Japanese literature considered one of the earliest examples of a novel, and is still widely read and studied today.

• • •

The first book to be printed using a printing press was the Gutenberg Bible in 1455. This revolutionary printing method made it possible for books to be mass-produced for the first time, allowing for the widespread dissemination of knowledge and ideas.

• • •

The Odyssey by Homer is considered one of the earliest and most important epic poems in Western literature. It is believed to have been written around the 8th century BCE, and features the story of the Greek hero Odysseus and his journey home after the Trojan War.

Edgar Allan Poe, the famous American author and poet was also a master of cryptography. He once challenged his readers to crack a code he had hidden in one of his stories, which was not deciphered until over 50 years later.

• • •

Children's and Young Adult literature is a rapidly growing segment of the book market, making up about 30% of all books sold in the US and around the world, with the *Harry Potter* series, *Hunger Games*, and *Divergent* series as the most popular books.

• • •

The concept of the "dystopian" society is often used in literature to reflect the ills and issues of contemporary society. George Orwell's *1984* and

Aldous Huxley's *Brave New World* are considered to be classic examples of dystopian literature.
The earliest known cave paintings are believed to be over 40,000 years old and are located in the Lascaux caves in France.

• • •

The Mona Lisa, a painting by Leonardo da Vinci, is considered one of the world's most famous paintings. It is also believed to be the most valuable, with a current estimated worth of over $1 billion.

• • •

The world's largest sculpture made entirely of recycled materials is "Goddess of the Mediterranean," by Eduardo Sanson. The sculpture is made of recycled materials, such as car parts, and stands 50 feet tall.

The first photograph ever taken was by Joseph Nicéphore Niépce in 1827. The photograph, named "View from the Window at Le Gras," is a picture of a country landscape.

• • •

The world's oldest known sculpture is a female figurine found in Germany, that is believed to be over 35,000 years old.

• • •

The oldest known painting in the world is a rock painting of a wild pig, it was found in Indonesia and is believed to be around 45,000 years old.

The sculpture of Christ the Redeemer in Rio de Janeiro, Brazil, is the largest art deco statue in the world, it stands at 98 ft (30 m) tall, including its pedestal, and its arms stretch 92 ft (28 m) wide.

• • •

The painting known as "Night Watch" by Rembrandt is actually called "The Militia Company of Captain Frans Banning Cocq," but it is widely known as Night Watch. It's one of the most famous paintings at Amsterdam's Rijksmuseum.

• • •

The term "selfie" was first used in a 2002 Australian online forum to describe a photograph taken of oneself. It wasn't until nearly a decade later that the term became popular and widely used in the digital age.

Banksy, the anonymous England-based street artist, political activist, and film director, is known for his controversial and thought-provoking works. Some of his works have sold for millions at auctions, but he also sometimes goes to great lengths to shred his own paintings moments after they've been sold.

• • •

The Sistine Chapel ceiling in the Vatican, painted by Michelangelo, is one of the most famous and iconic works of art in the world. It took the artist four years to complete and it depicts scenes from the book of Genesis.

• • •

The earliest known sculpture of the human form was found in the Czech Republic and is believed to be around 29,000 years old. It's a small, carved ivory figurine of a female.

The first use of the paint tube was patented by John Goffe Rand in 1841, revolutionising the way artists work, allowing them to work outdoors and to mix paint on a palette.

• • •

Salvador Dalí's famous painting "The Persistence of Memory" features melting watches, which symbolise the fluidity and instability of time.

• • •

The Italian artist Sandro Botticelli's famous painting "The Birth of Venus" is one of the best-known paintings of the Renaissance period. It can be seen at the Uffizi Gallery in Florence, Italy.

• • •

"The Scream," by Edvard Munch, was stolen from the National Gallery in Oslo in 2004 and recovered in 2006.

The world's highest-resolution photograph is the "Blackbird" photograph, taken by Fong Qi Wei; it's a composite of a staggering 238,000 individual photographs.

• • •

The word "set" has the most definitions in the English language, with over 430.

• • •

The longest word in the English language, according to the Oxford English Dictionary, is *pneumonoultramicroscopicsilicovolcanoconiosis*, a lung disease caused by inhaling very fine silica dust.

• • •

Andy Warhol's works continue to command high prices, with 11 of his pieces selling for a combined $81.4 million in 2023.

Two artworks sold for more than $100 million in 2023: Picasso's "Femme à la montre" and Klimt's "Dame mit Fächer."

• • •

A Rembrandt masterpiece, once sold for less than $15,800 as a work from the "circle" of Rembrandt, was later identified as genuine and valued at $18 million.

• • •

In 2023, the art world was abuzz when a stolen Vincent van Gogh painting, taken in 2020, was miraculously recovered. The 1884 masterpiece was anonymously left outside the residence of art crime expert Arthur Brand, wrapped in a nondescript blue Ikea bag.

Sources

Oxford Dictionary (2023). 2023. *Oxford Dictionary.* https://www.oed.com/dictionary/bridezilla_n?tab=meaning_and_use&tl=true

"Which English Words End With -Mt? | Lexico.Com". 2022. *Lexico Dictionaries | English.* https://www.lexico.com/explore/words-ending-with-mt.

"Green Eggs And Ham - Wikipedia". 2023. *En.Wikipedia.Org.* https://en.wikipedia.org/wiki/Green_Eggs_and_Ham.

"Freelancer - Wikipedia". 2022. *En.Wikipedia.Org.* https://en.wikipedia.org/wiki/Freelancer#Etymology.

"15 Behind-The-Scenes Drama You Didn't Know About 'Harry Potter'". 2017. *Thethings.* https://www.thethings.com/15-behind-the-scenes-drama-you-didnt-know-about-harry-potter/.

"Mark Twain - Wikipedia". 2017. *En.Wikipedia.Org.* https://en.wikipedia.org/wiki/Mark_Twain.

"What's The Rarest Letter Of The Alphabet?". 2016. *The Rarest Letter Of The Alphabet | Grammarly.* https://www.grammarly.com/blog/rarest-letter-in-english/.

"This Is The 'Harry Potter' Synopsis Publishers Rejected 20 Years Ago". 2017. *Huffpost UK.* https://www.huffpost.com/entry/harry-potter-synopsis-jk-rowling_n_59f1e294e4b043885915a95c.

"Reading, Chess May Help Fight Alzheimer's". 2022. *ABC News.* https://abcnews.go.com/Health/story?id=117588&page=1.

"750 Million Adults Around The World Cannot Read A Story Like This One". 2022. *Theirworld*. https://theirworld.org/news/750-million-adults-around-the-world-cannot-read-a-story-like-this-one.

"Most People Balancing Books On Their Heads Simultaneously". 2022. *Guinness World Records*. https://www.guinnessworldrecords.com/world-records/most-people-balancing-books-on-their-heads/.

Hammond, Claudia. 2022. **"Does Reading Fiction Make Us Better People?"**. *Bbc.Com*. https://www.bbc.com/future/article/20190523-does-reading-fiction-make-us-better-people.

"Mark Twain Wrote The First Book Ever Written With A Typewriter". 2022. *Open Culture*. https://www.openculture.com/2013/03/mark_twain_wrote_the_first_book_ever_written_with_a_typewriter.html.

"Shakespeare's Influence - Wikipedia". 2011. *En.Wikipedia.Org*. https://en.wikipedia.org/wiki/Shakespeare%27s_influence#Vocabulary.

"J.K. Rowling". 2023. *Forbes*. https://www.forbes.com/profile/jk-rowling/?sh=239238cc3aeb.

"Harper Lee - Wikipedia". 2022. *En.Wikipedia.Org*. https://en.wikipedia.org/wiki/Harper_Lee.

"Wendy - Wikipedia". 2022. *En.Wikipedia.Org*. https://en.wikipedia.org/wiki/Wendy.

"Look Inside The Rare Leonardo Da Vinci Notebook That Bill Gates Paid More Than $30 Million For". 2023. *Business Insider*. https://www.businessinsider.com/look-inside-the-codex-leicester-which-bill-gates-bought-for-30-million-2015-7

"Five Fascinating Facts About Dr Seuss". 2015. *Interesting Literature*. https://interestingliterature.com/2015/03/five-fascinating-facts-about-dr-seuss/.

Steinmetz, Katy. 2022. **“Why F. Scott Fitzgerald Is All Over The Dictionary | TIME.Com”**. *TIME.Com.* https://newsfeed.time.com/2013/05/08/why-f-scott-fitzgerald-is-all-over-the-dictionary/.

“The Inventing Room - Roald Dahl”. 2022. *Roalddahl.Com.* https://www.roalddahl.com/roald-dahl/archive/archive-highlights/the-inventing-room.

“DATA STORY: Indians Spend More Time Reading Than Anyone Else In The World”. 2022. *Moneycontrol.* https://www.moneycontrol.com/news/trends/data-story-indians-spend-more-time-reading-than-anyone-else-in-the-world-2425835.html.

“J.K. Rowling Wrote One of the Most Important Parts of Harry Potter On An Airplane Vomit Bag”. 2017. *Bustle.* https://www.bustle.com/p/jk-rowling-reveals-she-came-up-with-hogwarts-houses-on-the-back-of-airplane-vomit-bag-7607721

“List Of Best-Selling Books - Wikipedia”. 2023. *En.Wikipedia.Org.* https://en.wikipedia.org/wiki/List_of_best-selling_books.
“The Ghost Club - Wikipedia”. 2022. *En.Wikipedia.Org.* https://en.wikipedia.org/wiki/The_Ghost_Club.

“Of Mice And Men - Wikipedia”. 2022. *En.Wikipedia.Org.* https://en.wikipedia.org/wiki/Of_Mice_and_Men.

Rodger, James. 2015. **“Shakespeare Day 2015: 10 Facts You Didn’t Know About William Shakespeare”**. *Coventrylive.* https://www.coventrytelegraph.net/whats-on/whats-on-news/shakespeare-day-2015-10-facts-9091035.

“To Kill A Mockingbird - Wikipedia”. 2023. *En.Wikipedia.Org.* https://en.wikipedia.org/wiki/To_Kill_a_Mockingbird.

Anderson, Hephzibah. 2022. **“The Dark Side Of Roald Dahl”.** *Bbc.Com.* https://www.bbc.com/culture/article/20160912-the-dark-side-of-roald-dahl.

"Pride And Prejudice - Wikipedia". 2023. *En.Wikipedia.Org*. https://en.wikipedia.org/wiki/Pride_and_Prejudice.

"Who Is Silas Tomkyn Comberbache?". 2010. *Samueltaylorcoleridge. Blogspot.Com*. http://samueltaylorcoleridge.blogspot.com/2010/12/who-is-silas-tomkyn-comberbache.html.

"Market Recap 2023." 2023. *Artsy*. https://www.artsy.net/article/artsy-editorial-art-market-recap-2023

"117 Fascinating Finds Revealed in 2023." 2023. *Smithsonian*. Retrieved from https://www.smithsonianmag.com/history/117-fascinating-finds-revealed-in-2023-180983491/

Sports & Leisure

Ready to dive into the world of backflips and board games? Whether you're the type who gets pumped up for the big game or you're more into strategising over a game of chess, this chapter's got you covered.

From the adrenaline rush of scoring a try to the satisfaction of a perfectly placed LEGO brick, there's a thrill in every activity. We're exploring the wide world of sports and leisure, where every hobby scores big.

Buckle up; it's game time!

Novak Djokovic made history by winning his 23rd Grand Slam title at the US Open 2023, surpassing the previous record held by Rafael Nadal and becoming the most decorated male tennis player in Grand Slam history.

•••

Tigst Assefa set a new world record in the marathon, becoming the only woman in history to run a marathon in under two hours and 12 minutes, finishing the BMW Berlin Marathon in 2:11:53.

•••

The term pound cake originated from the pound of each of the four ingredients needed to make it.

The ancient Greeks held the first Olympic Games in 776 BCE to honor the god Zeus. Athletes competed in events such as running, jumping, and wrestling.

• • •

The modern Olympic Games were first held in Athens, Greece, in 1896. Since then, they have been held every four years, except during World War I , World War II and the COVID-19 pandemic.

• • •

The fastest recorded speed of a fastball in baseball is 105.1 mph, thrown by Cincinnati Reds player Aroldis Chapman in 2010.

• • •

The first FIFA World Cup was held in Uruguay in 1930. Uruguay defeated Argentina 4-2 in the final in front of a crowd of 93,000 spectators.

The Tour de France, the world's most famous bike race, was first held in 1903. The race covers more than 2,200 miles and lasts for three weeks.

• • •

The first recorded basketball game was played in a YMCA gym in Springfield, Massachusetts, in 1891. James Naismith, a Canadian physical education instructor, invented the game as a way to keep his students active during the winter months.

• • •

The first recorded game of American football was played in 1869 between two college teams, Rutgers and Princeton. The game was similar to soccer and rugby, with 25 players on each team.

The Boston Marathon, first run in 1897, is the oldest marathon in the world. It is run on the third Monday of April, and it's considered one of the world's most prestigious marathons.

• • •

Did you know that skydivers played Scrabble during a 13,000-foot drop to celebrate the game's 60th birthday in 2008? They used a specially reinforced wooden board and super-sticky adhesive pieces to keep the game intact mid-air.

• • •

The first recorded game of golf, played in Scotland in the 15th century, was quite different from the modern game. Players used a stick to hit a pebble instead of a ball, and the object was to hit the pebble into a series of holes in as few strokes as possible.

Wimbledon was originally staged to raise funds for croquet equipment. The All-England Club, founded primarily as a croquet club in 1868, introduced lawn tennis as a way to finance a pony-drawn roller for croquet lawns. The inaugural tennis championship in 1877 effectively transformed the club's focus towards tennis, leading to "croquet" being dropped from the club name (though it was later reinstated).

• • •

The first official Ryder Cup trophy, which is 17 inches tall and weighs four pounds, was modeled to resemble British golfing great Abe Mitchell. This is a nod to Samuel Ryder's (who the Cup is named after) admiration for Mitchell, who was not only a legendary golfer but also Ryder's personal golf instructor.

The America's Cup began in 1851 and is considered the oldest active trophy in international sports. It is a sailing competition between yachts representing different countries, and the winners get to choose the location of the next competition.

• • •

One of the longest-running sports rivalries is the "El Clásico" between the football teams Real Madrid and FC Barcelona, which have been competing against each other since 1902.

• • •

In 2022, Lewis Hamilton's streak of 15 consecutive years with at least one win in a Formula One season came to an end, as he failed to win any race. Meanwhile, Max Verstappen emerged as a top contender, winning an impressive 15 races, setting a new record for the most wins by a driver in a single year in Formula One history.

Morocco made history in the 2022 World Cup by becoming the first team from Africa to reach the semifinals.

• • •

The Boston Red Sox went 86 years without winning a World Series, from 1918 to 2004, earning them the nickname "the Curse of the Bambino."

• • •

The highest ever recorded score in a professional game of ten-pin bowling is a perfect score of 300, which can be achieved by hitting all ten pins in each of the ten frames.

• • •

The world's oldest known recipe is for beer, dating back to ancient Sumeria around 4000 BC.

Some winemakers in France and Italy bury their wine bottles underground for months or years to enhance flavor, a technique known as "winemaking subterranea" or "vin du terroir."

• • •

A bank manager from Arkansas stumbled across a 9.07-carat diamond in Crater of Diamonds State Park in 2020, the second-largest ever found there. It is estimated to be worth between $123,000-$1.8 million.

• • •

Hawaiian pizza was created in 1962 in Ontario, Canada, by Greek immigrant Sam Panopoulos.

A groundbreaking study found that boyfriends do a lot more housework than husbands.

• • •

The silhouette on the NBA logo was modelled after Jerry West.

• • •

Do you know what's inside a Kit Kat? More Kit Kat! That's right, Kit Kats that are damaged during production are ground up and go between the wafers inside, along with cocoa and sugar.

• • •

The Hawaiian islands are the biggest consumers of SPAM in the world. Hawaiians consume over seven million cans of SPAM a year. You'll even find SPAM on the menu at high-end restaurants.

After setting off in June 2019 from England, two women became the fastest people to cycle around the world on a tandem bike. They completed their journey in 263 days, 8 hours and 7 minutes.

• • •

After the 2005 tsunami in Indonesia, Cristiano Ronaldo sponsored a 7-year-old boy who was spotted wearing a Portugal jersey. He went on to be signed by Lisbon in 2015.

• • •

You can burn 100 calories per hour just standing and doing nothing.

• • •

The Cleveland Browns are the only team to neither play in nor host a Super Bowl.

The longest game of cricket lasted 12 days. The game between England and South Africa ended without a winner as the English team had to catch their boat home.

•••

At the first modern Olympic Games, winners were awarded silver medals, an olive branch and a diploma.

•••

The most common number of dimples on a golf ball is 336.

•••

Formula 1 drivers lose around 4 kg (8.8 lb) of body weight and 3 litres (0.79 gallons) of water after each race.

Between 1912-1948 art used to be an Olympic sport. There were competitions for sculpture, music, literature, painting and architecture. Medals were awarded to works of art inspired by sport.

• • •

During the Super Bowl halftime, more toilets flush than at any other time of the year in the USA.

• • •

In July 2020, a LeBron James trading card sold for a record-breaking $1.845 million.

• • •

Belinda Clark was the first person to score a double century in a cricket One Day International.

The last Olympic Games to give out medals made entirely of gold were in 1912.

• • •

The world's most wanted hacker was himself hacked and subsequently arrested because his password was his cat's name plus 123.

• • •

Three Olympic Games have been held in countries that no longer exist.

• • •

The last time the Chicago Cubs won a World Series, the Ottoman Empire existed.

Adidas and Puma were founded by two brothers: Adolph and Rudolf Dassler. They were huge rivals.

• • •

The highest paid sports star in 2023 was Cristiano Ronaldo, who earned a whopping $275 million. In second place was golfer Jon Rahm with $203 million.

• • •

Only one in 3,332 US high school football players make it into the NFL.

• • •

The first toy to ever be advertised on television was Mr Potato Head, in 1952.

Liechtenstein has taken part in the most Olympic Games without winning any medals.

• • •

Shaquille O'Neal has a doctorate in education. He wrote his thesis on humour in the workplace.

• • •

Joe Gibbs is the only coach to have won the Super Bowl with three different quarterbacks.

• • •

Major League Baseball umpires are required to wear black underwear while on the job in case they split their pants.

Researchers from Texas A&M University are developing a novel amino acid alternative curing system for cured meat products. This new method aims to eliminate the need for direct or indirect addition of sodium nitrite, which has raised health concerns.

• • •

Punters have the longest average NFL careers at 4.87 years.

• • •

Shohei Ohtani signed a reported 10-year, $700 million contract with the Los Angeles Dodgers in 2023, the largest deal in professional sports history.

The bushes in Super Mario Bros. were just recoloured clouds.

• • •

The popular iOS game, Clash of Clans, makes an incredible 1.5 million dollars per day.

• • •

There are more possible iterations of chess than there are atoms in the entire universe.

• • •

It wasn't until 1907 that Major League baseball teams started using numbers on their jerseys for identification.

The development of lab-grown or cultured meat is gaining attention as a potential solution to address the environmental and animal welfare concerns of traditional meat production. Some experts predict that lab-grown meat may make up nearly a quarter of global meat consumption by 2035.

• • •

Babe Ruth wore a cabbage leaf under his cap to keep him cool, and he changed it over every two innings.

• • •

China didn't win an Olympic medal until 1984. However, at the 2004 Beijing Olympics, they won 100 medals.

The longest game of chess that is theoretically possible has just over 5,000 moves.

• • •

The folding chessboard was invented by a priest who was forbidden to play chess. The priest found a way around it by making a folding chessboard. When folded together and put on a bookshelf, it simply looks like two books.

• • •

Arts and crafts activities, as well as cooking/baking, have seen a surge in popularity in 2023, especially among men, with 40% of men reporting engaging in these hobbies in the past 6 months.

Track athletes are most likely to break records late in the day when their body temperatures are highest.

• • •

The word "checkmate" in chess comes from the Persian phrase "Shah Mat," which means "the King is dead."

• • •

After his jerseys were stolen from the visitors' locker room when the team was on the road against Orlando Magic, Michael Jordan had to wear a No. 12 jersey.

Michael Jordan made $300 million in 2023, a large portion of which still comes from his shoe deal with Nike. He earned more than 3 times the amount in 2023 than he earned in his entire NBA career.

• • •

It takes 3,000 cows to supply the NFL with enough leather for a year's supply of footballs.

• • •

Alaska is the only state to have never sent a school to the NCAA Tournament.

• • •

The first chessboard with alternating light and dark squares appeared in Europe in 1090.

Golf balls can reach speeds of over 170 mph (273 km/h).

• • •

Pittsburgh is the only American city with three sports teams that wear the same colours.

• • •

While museums are appreciated by the majority of consumers, with 81% in the US and 79% in the UK acknowledging their appeal, there is a gap between appreciation and actual visitation, with over half of consumers rarely or never visiting museums.

• • •

Kareem Abdul-Jabbar, the NBA's all-time leading scorer (38,387 points), collects rugs.

Federer can be typed entirely with the left-hand side of a keyboard.

• • •

While he was practising baseball, Bulls and White Sox owner Jerry Reinsdorf was still paying Michael Jordan his $4 million annual basketball salary.

• • •

Four presidents have been on the cover of Sports Illustrated magazine: Bill Clinton, Ronald Reagan, John F. Kennedy and Gerald Ford.

• • •

Ronnie O'Sullivan became the oldest winner of the 2023 UK Snooker Championship, adding to his record as the youngest winner.

The average lifespan of an MLB baseball is five to seven pitches.

• • •

Weight is more important for race car drivers than it is for runway models.

• • •

Manchester City's men's team completed a historic treble, winning the FA Cup, Premier League, and UEFA Champions League in 2023.

• • •

The world's oldest bodybuilder was crowned in 2023. Jim Arrington, now aged 91, was crowned the world's oldest bodybuilder by Guinness World Records when he turned 83. Seven years later, he was still getting his swole on, so Guinness declared him the reigning record holder.

In 2023, the ancient Mesoamerican ballgame Ōllamaliztli (or Ulama) experienced a revival in Mexico, with new courts being built and regional tournaments attracting international attention.

• • •

2023 data revealed that a quarter of consumers have never visited a theme park, with the figure rising to 33% in Europe and 30% in North America. However, in the APAC region and the UAE, only 5% of consumers said they don't visit theme parks.

• • •

During World War II, Wimbledon's Centre Court was bombed by the Nazis in 1940, destroying 1,200 seats.

Kathrine Switzer became the first woman to run the Boston Marathon as a numbered entrant in 1967. During her run, an official tried to physically remove her from the race because it was a men-only event, but she persisted and finished the marathon.

•••

Junko Tabei from Japan became the first woman to reach the summit of Mount Everest in 1975. Despite an avalanche during her expedition that left her buried for a time, Tabei persisted and achieved this historic feat.

Sources

"Pound Cake - Wikipedia". 2022. *En.Wikipedia.Org.* https://en.wikipedia.org/wiki/Pound_cake.

"Lego - Wikipedia". 2022. *En.Wikipedia.Org.* https://en.wikipedia.org/wiki/Lego.

Badenhausen, Kurt. 2022. **"Naomi Osaka Is The Highest-Paid Female Athlete Ever, Topping Serena Williams"**. *Forbes*. https://www.forbes.com/sites/kurt-badenhausen/2020/05/22/naomi-osaka-is-the-highest-paid-female-athlete-ever-topping-serena-williams/?sh=2beba9441fd3.

"Does Jerry West Get Royalties For Being The NBA Logo?". 2015. *Mental-floss.Com.* https://www.mentalfloss.com/article/63937/does-jerry-west-get-royalties-being-nba-logo.

"Martunis - Wikipedia". 2022. *En.Wikipedia.Org.* https://en.wikipedia.org/wiki/Martunis.

"List Of Super Bowl Champions - Wikipedia". 2022. *En.Wikipedia.Org.* https://en.wikipedia.org/wiki/List_of_Super_Bowl_champions.

"Athens 1896 Olympic Medal Table - Gold, Silver & Bronze". 2022. *Olympics.Com.* https://olympics.com/en/olympic-games/athens-1896/medals.

"Q & A: How Many Dimples On A Golf Ball | Department Of Physics | University Of Illinois At Urbana-Champaign". 2022. *Van.Physics.Illinois.Edu.* https://van.physics.illinois.edu/qa/listing.php?id=947.

"The Human Element – Why The Singapore GP Represents The Biggest Physical Test Of The Season - Motorsport Technology". 2019. *Motorsport Technology.* https://motorsport.tech/formula-1/the-human-element-why-the-singapore-gp-represents-the-biggest-physical-test-of-the-season.

"Timeless Test - Wikipedia". 2022. *En.Wikipedia.Org.* https://en.wikipedia.org/wiki/Timeless_Test.

"The Super Bowl Of Toilets". 2015. *The Daily Beast.* https://www.thedaily-beast.com/the-super-bowl-of-toilets.

"Belinda Clark Scored ODI Cricket's First Double Hundred". 2022. *Inshorts - Stay Informed*. https://inshorts.com/en/news/belinda-clark-scored-odi-crickets-first-double-hundred-1513408037520.

"Gold Medal - Wikipedia". 2017. *En.Wikipedia.Org*. https://en.wikipedia.org/wiki/Gold_medal.

"10 Facts About SPAM That You Might Not Have Known". 2017. *Foodbeast.Com*. https://www.foodbeast.com/news/10-facts-about-spam-that-you-might-not-have-known/.

"What's Really In The Middle Of A Kit Kat? The Answer Is Blowing Our Minds". 2019. *TODAY.Com*. https://www.today.com/food/kit-kat-bars-are-made-ground-kit-kats-t106777.

"Art Competitions At The Summer Olympics - Wikipedia". 2013. *En.Wikipedia.Org*. https://en.wikipedia.org/wiki/Art_competitions_at_the_Summer_Olympics.

"Past Countries At The Olympics". 2022. *Topendsports.Com*. https://www.topendsports.com/events/summer/countries/countries-past.htm.

"Study: Boyfriends Outdo Husbands On Housework". 2007. *Newsweek*. https://www.newsweek.com/study-boyfriends-outdo-husbands-housework-100089.

"The Last Time The Cubs Won, The Ottoman Empire Still Existed". 2016. *Huffpost UK*. https://www.huffpost.com/entry/chicago-cubs-ottoman-empire-world-series_n_58179ce9e4b0390e69d1e30b.

"Puma And Adidas' Rivalry Has Divided A Small German Town For 70 Years — Here's What It Looks Like Now". 2022. *Business Insider*. https://www.businessinsider.com/how-puma-and-adidas-rivalry-divided-their-founding-town-for-70-years-2018-10.

"Floyd Mayweather Net Worth 2022: Age, Height, Wife, Children, Bio, Wiki & Facts | Raphael Saadiq". 2019. *Raphaelsaadiq.Com*. https://www.raphaelsaadiq.com/biography-wiki-age-height-net-worth/boxer/floyd-mayweather-2019-2020-2021-2022/.

"Getting Into The Game | NFL Football Operations". 2022. *Operations.Nfl. Com.* https://operations.nfl.com/journey-to-the-nfl/the-next-generation-of-nfl-stars/getting-into-the-game/.

"Mr. Potato Head - Wikipedia". 2021. *En.Wikipedia.Org.* https://en.wikipedia.org/wiki/Mr._Potato_Head.

"Liechtenstein At The 2016 Summer Olympics - Wikipedia". 2022. *En.Wikipedia.Org.* https://en.wikipedia.org/wiki/Liechtenstein_at_the_2016_Summer_Olympics.

"Shaquille O'neal Becomes Receives Doctorate Degree". 2022. *ABC News.* https://abcnews.go.com/blogs/headlines/2012/05/shaquille-oneal-earns-ph-d-in-education.

"Joe Gibbs | Pro Football Hall Of Fame Official Site". 2022. *Pfhof.* https://www.profootballhof.com/players/joe-gibbs/.

"MLB Umpires Must Wear Black Underwear, In Case They Split Their Pants. - South Florida Reporter". 2019. *South Florida Reporter.* https://southfloridareporter.com/mlb-umpires-must-wear-black-underwear-in-case-they-split-their-pants/.

"How Long Is The Average Career Of An NFL Player?". 2022. *Career Trend.* https://careertrend.com/how-long-is-the-average-career-of-an-nfl-player-3032896.html.

"The Top-Grossing Iphone App Makes A Whopping $1.5 Million A Day". 2022. *Business Insider.* https://www.businessinsider.com/clash-of-clans-earns-15-million-a-day-as-top-grossing-app-2015-6.

"Uniform Number (Major League Baseball) - Wikipedia". 2022. *En.Wikipedia.Org.* https://en.wikipedia.org/wiki/Uniform_number_(Major_League_Baseball).

"Babe Ruth". 2022. *Biography.* https://www.biography.com/athlete/babe-ruth.

"China At The Olympics - Wikipedia". 2022. *En.Wikipedia.Org.* https://en.wikipedia.org/wiki/China_at_the_Olympics.

"The Longest Possible Chess Game". 2007. *Chess.Com.* https://www.chess.com/blog/kurtgodden/the-longest-possible-chess-game.

"Origins Of Chess". 2008. *Chess.Com.* https://www.chess.com/article/view/origins-of-chess.

Pumerantz, Zack. 2022. **"100 Random Sports Facts You Never Knew"**. *Bleacher Report.* https://bleacherreport.com/articles/950303-100-random-sports-facts-you-never-knew.

"Checkmate - Wikipedia". 2022. *En.Wikipedia.Org.* https://en.wikipedia.org/wiki/Checkmate.

"Swing Speed vs Ball Speed". 2022. *Golftips.Golfweek.Usatoday.Com.* https://golftips.golfweek.usatoday.com/swing-speed-vs-ball-speed-1637.html.

"Sports In Pittsburgh - Wikipedia". 2022. *En.Wikipedia.Org.* https://en.wikipedia.org/wiki/Sports_in_Pittsburgh.

"Here's Where Kareem Abdul-Jabbar Is Selling His Amazing Rug Collection". 2016. *Crain's Chicago Business.* https://www.chicagobusiness.com/article/20160212/NEWS07/160219923/kareem-abdul-jabbar-selling-rug-collection-at-minasian-rug-co-in-evanston.

"Hoop Dreams". 1995. *Newsweek.* https://www.newsweek.com/hoop-dreams-180618.

"Presidents On The Cover". 2022. *Sports Illustrated.* https://www.si.com/more-sports/2008/11/04/04presidents-on-the-cover#gid=ci0255c8caa0082515&pid=jo hn-amp-jacqueline-kennedy.

"Fact Of The Day: Average Life Span Of A Major League Baseball". 2022. *MLB.Com.* https://www.mlb.com/news/fact-of-the-day-average-life-span-of-a-major-league-baseball/c-35024016

"8 Things You May Not Know About Wimbledon." (n.d.). **History.com.** https://www.history.com/news/wimbledon-tennis-tournament-facts

Hooper, B. *2023.* **"Watch: World's oldest bodybuilder going strong at 90."** https://www.upi.com/Odd_News/2023/07/19/Guinness-World-Records-oldest-bodybuilder/5761689787428/

Rizzo, C. *2022*. **"Flight Attendant Reveals the Best Time to Visit the Airplane Restroom."** https://www.travelandleisure.com/airlines-airports/best-time-to-go-airplane-bathroom

"Ulama (game)". *2024.* https://en.wikipedia.org/wiki/Ulama_(game)

Knight, R. *2023*. **"This has been 2023 in sport - and the top 25 most memorable moments."** https://www.mirror.co.uk/sport/top-25-sporting-moments-2023-31727130

Joseph, S. *2023*. **"This is what happened in sport during 2023."** https://edition.cnn.com/2023/12/23/sport/2023-in-sport-biggest-stories-spt-intl/index.html

Henderson, B. *2023*. **"Top Food Safety Innovations of 2023."** https://www.food-safety.com/articles/9130-top-food-safety-innovations-of-2023

Sarah. *2023*. **"2023 Food Tech Trends: Key Factors Shaping Future Innovation."** https://libereat.com/2023/03/food-tech-trends-2023/

"Leisure and Entertainment: 2023 - US - 2023 : Consumer market research report: Mintel.com." *2023.* https://store.mintel.com/us/report/leisure-and-entertainment-2023-us-2023/

"Leisure and entertainment – trends and insights roundup for 2023." *2023.* https://business.yougov.com/content/48240-leisure-and-entertainment-trends-and-insights-roundup-for-2023

Lw. *2024*. **"Cristiano Ronaldo was the highest-paid athlete in the world in 2023 - What was his income?"** https://www.marca.com/en/football/2024/02/08/65c45276268e3ec7398b456e.html

"Novak Djokovic reaches record 23 grand slam titles after French Open final win." *2023.* https://www.theguardian.com/sport/2023/jun/11/novak-djokovic-casper-ruud-french-open-23-grand-slam-titles-tennis.

"12 Women's Sports Records Set in 2023." *2023.* https://www.togethxr.com/blogs/guides/2023-womens-sports-records

Latham, S. 2022. **"22 Things You Didn't Know About Your Favorite Board Games."** https://blog.cheapism.com/board-game-trivia/

“Kathrine Switzer.” 2024. https://en.wikipedia.org/wiki/Kathrine_Switzer

“Junko Tabei.” 2024. Retrieved from https://en.wikipedia.org/wiki/Junko_Tabei

Miscellaneous & Bizarre

We have thousands of facts up our sleeve... and some of them are just too bizarre to fit in another category. From delightful quirks to astonishing truths, it's the perfect ending to the book.

So, dig in and enjoy.

As whiskey is distilled, approximately 20 per cent of it evaporates. Whiskey distillers call this "the angels share".

• • •

A single strand of spaghetti is called a spaghetto, and a single ravioli is a raviolo. The -i ending we are used to seeing indicates the plural in Italian.

• • •

Before Heinz popularised tomato ketchup, mushroom ketchup was a thing. British colonists even brought mushroom ketchup to the United States in the 1770s.

It has become increasingly normal for people to wear pyjamas in public. In fact, in January 2010, a Tesco supermarket in Cardiff started a ban on customers wearing pyjamas to their store.

• • •

The different colours of Froot Loops cereal all taste the same—they're not individual flavours.

• • •

It's impossible to hum while holding your nose. Try it!

• • •

The inventor of candy floss was a dentist.

In 1927, Santa Claus received a pilot's license from the US Government.

• • •

An Australian man tried to sell New Zealand on eBay. However, bidding was stopped at $3,000 when eBay caught on.

• • •

The black box in an aeroplane is actually orange.

• • •

Japanese scientists discovered that some mammals (possibly including humans!) can breathe through their anuses.

The small hole in the bottom of a padlock lets water drain out in case it rains.

• • •

In 1992, nearly 30,000 rubber ducks fell off of a cargo ship and people are still finding them today.

• • •

Fruit stickers are edible. The paper and the glue are controlled by the FDA.

• • •

In 2014, two research scientists in Antarctica matched each other on Tinder. They were 45 minutes away from each other by helicopter.

The expiration date written on a water bottle is for the bottle, not for the water inside. Over time, the plastic can leach toxic chemicals into the water.

• • •

It is not moths that are eating your clothing, but their larvae. They are particularly keen on keratin-based fibres such as wool and cashmere.

• • •

Humans are the only species that enjoy eating spicy food.

• • •

In 1986, Apple had its own clothing and lifestyle brand. Despite the outrageously bright colours and a matching suite of accessories, unfortunately, it didn't take off.

To find out if cranberries are ripe, growers drop them to see if they can bounce over several wooden barriers. If they bounce, they're ripe.

• • •

The world's smallest inhabited island is in New York State. It's called 'Just Enough Room' and has a small house and a tree on it.

• • •

To pass your exam to become a taxi driver in London you must remember 320 routes, 25,000 streets, and 20,000 sights—without GPS!

• • •

There's a type of bridge called the 'squirrel bridge', which lets squirrels and other small animals safely cross busy highways. The first one was built in Longview, Washington.

Bubble wrap was originally meant to be a textured wallpaper. It was invented accidentally in 1957 by engineer Al Fielding and inventor Marc Chavannes by sealing two shower curtains together in a way that captured bubbles of air.

• • •

Doritos are great for using as kindling on fires as they are highly flammable and burn for a long time.

• • •

German chocolate cake has nothing to do with Germany. It was named after an American baker called Samuel German.

• • •

A chef's hat is called a toque and has exactly 100 pleats. Toque is Arabic for 'hat'.

The noun for both nephews and nieces is ‘neblings’.

• • •

There is only a 1:1461 chance of a baby being born on February 29th.

• • •

Boston has the highest number of berry-eaters in the United States.

• • •

Stop signs were yellow for 30 years. However, this ended in 1954 when they invented a red paint that wouldn’t fade in the sun.

The original idea for tea bags was to remove the tea leaves from the bags and put them into metal infusers, but people misunderstood and started brewing their tea straight from the bags, so it stuck.

•••

In April 2020, the Pentagon officially released videos showing UFO's, the first time the government has done so.

•••

More people die from selfies than shark attacks.

•••

A police officer's life was saved by a woman who he had put in jail eight years prior. She wanted to show her appreciation for saving her from drug addiction, so she donated her kidney to him.

If you have an itchy throat, scratching your ear can help calm it down.

• • •

Between 65-81 per cent of people can curl their tongue into a tube, with women more likely to be able to do it than men.

• • •

Millennials are estimated to return more than 75 per cent of the clothes they purchase online, while Baby Boomers return less than 50 per cent.

• • •

The dot above the “i” is called a tittle.

“Vanity sizing” is the method some brands use to make customers feel slimmer than they are, by making clothes bigger than the label size suggests. Standard clothing sizes were scrapped in the US in 1983, so this is perfectly legal.

• • •

Diet soda has been shown to increase hunger.

• • •

You can find all the letters in the word ‘typewriter’ on one line of your keyboard.

• • •

A penny doubled every day becomes over five million dollars in just 30 days.

The number 2,520 can be divided by 1, 2, 3, 4, 5, 6, 7, 8, 9 and 10 without having a fractional leftover.

• • •

The infinity sign is called a lemniscate.

• • •

Months that begin on a Sunday will always have a Friday the 13th.

• • •

It is possible to turn a person's ashes into a diamond.

• • •

Over 95 per cent of people who have lived to be over 110 are women.

There are more plastic flamingos in the USA than there are real ones.

• • •

The only 15 letter word that can be spelt without repeating a letter is “uncopyrightable”.

• • •

Fourteen squirrels were detained and charged with espionage on the Iranian border. They were allegedly carrying devices used to gather information.

• • •

If you are completely lost, head downhill. Downhill leads to water, which eventually leads to people.

If you wear headphones in your ears for just one hour it will increase your ear's bacteria by 700 times.

• • •

Dead people can get goosebumps.

• • •

The longest official place name in the world is Taumatawhakatangihangakoauauotamateapokaiwhenuakitanatahu, a hill in New Zealand.

• • •

If you find a lost driver's license in the USA you can just drop it into a mailbox and the postman will deliver it back to its owner.

To stay healthy you only technically have to have a shower once or twice a week. We do so more regularly for vanity reasons.

• • •

It is estimated that up to one billion birds die every year from smashing into windows.

• • •

A surfer once sued another surfer for 'stealing his wave'.

• • •

The Statue of Liberty wears a size 879 sandal.

• • •

Hurricanes with women's names kill more people than those with men's.

The face of a penny can hold approximately 30 drops of water.

• • •

No piece of paper can be folded in half more than 12 times.

• • •

In a set of 23 randomly chosen people, there is a 50 per cent probability of two people having the same birthday.

• • •

Nearly half of all US college students drop out before they get a degree.

The Maruyama Zoo in Japan spent four years trying to get two hyenas to mate before realising they were both males.

• • •

It takes approximately 66 days for a habit to stick.

• • •

Pogonophobia is the fear of beards.

• • •

People who regularly take naps tend to die younger than those who don't.

• • •

If you are a redhead you might be able to get a high school scholarship that is only for redheads!

In French, the word 'avocat' means both avocado and lawyer.

• • •

An American artist by the name of Pope. L has eaten entire issues of the Wall Street Journal and belly-crawled around the entirety of Manhattan. He refers to himself as a 'fisherman of social absurdity'.

• • •

Despite popular belief, urine does not cure jellyfish stings. It can actually make them worse.

• • •

Around a third of all murders in the US go unsolved.

Before Harry Houdini died, he left very detailed information about how he would contact his loved ones after his death.

• • •

McDonald's created the McRib in 1981 after the introduction of chicken nuggets were so popular they resulted in a chicken shortage.

• • •

There is a blind guy who can ride his bike in traffic using echolocation.

• • •

Fashion designer Karl Lagerfield had 300 iPods. He hired someone whose sole job was to take care of them.

It was illegal to sell sex toys in Texas until 2008. It is still illegal in Alabama.

• • •

Seventy-four per cent of American couples who were married in 2018 created a wedding website.

• • •

In 2012 in Sweden, a man named Peter Skyllberg managed to stay alive in his snowed-in car for two months by staying warm in his sleeping bag and eating snow.

• • •

There is a website that allows you to anonymously send animal poop to a person.

An Australian woman from Brisbane broke the Guinness World Record for "most cinema productions attended–same film" after watching Bohemian Rhapsody 107 times.

•••

The letter 'Q' is the only one that doesn't appear in any US state name.

•••

During the 1800s, Egyptians demonstrated their courage by placing their hands inside the mouths of crocodiles.

•••

In ancient Egypt, the death of a cat was a significant event for a family. They would mourn and shave off their eyebrows as a sign of grief. In some cases, they would even mummify their beloved cat as a tribute to their affection and loyalty.

During medieval times in Europe, it was believed that consuming the liver of a polar bear would give one strength and bravery.

•••

In ancient Greece, it was seen as a good omen to present a hard-boiled egg to the bride at her wedding ceremony to guarantee a fruitful union.

•••

In medieval England, a law was made that said all people aged 14 and older had to go to church on Sundays or they would be punished.

•••

If you point a laser at an aircraft in the USA you could go to prison for 20 years.

There is a single common ancestor behind blue eyes.

• • •

Since 1970, the National Library Service for the Blind and Physically Handicapped has been publishing Braille versions of Playboy magazine; it does not include pictures.

• • •

You may have more bones than you think! A study found that over 36% of people have "accessory bones" in their feet. These extra bones are commonly found near the wrist, ankle, foot, or neck and are small and pebble-like. Around 10% of adults have extra vertebrae in their spine, while others have cervical ribs, which can sometimes cause health issues.

In 2023, the Harrogate Autumn Flower Show featured the world's largest onion, a hefty specimen weighing just under 9 kg (20 pounds).

• • •

A hardboiled egg will spin smoothly, unlike its uncooked or soft-boiled counterparts.

• • •

The Barbie craze of 2023 saw the Alpha and Omega Funeral Home in El Salvador introduce pink Barbie-themed coffins, with ten individuals opting for them as their final resting places by early August.

• • •

An overdue library book, "An Elementary Treatise on Electricity" by James Clerk Maxwell, was returned to the New Bedford Free Public Library 119 years late in 2023, after being found in a donation pile at West Virginia University Libraries.

Chipotle announced the testing of a new robot named “Autocado” in 2023, designed to slice, core, and peel avocados, potentially halving the time it takes to prepare guacamole.

• • •

Apple’s iOS 17 update in fall 2023 finally refined autocorrect, allowing users to more accurately express themselves without unintended ‘ducking’ substitutions.

• • •

In 2023, Guinness recognized Cellato’s $6696 dessert as the world’s most expensive ice cream, crafted with ingredients like gold-leaf shavings, rare white truffle, Parmigiano Reggiano, and sake lees.

Japanese researchers discovered a novel use for disposable diapers in 2023, incorporating them into concrete for house construction, which could significantly benefit environmental sustainability and waste reduction.

• • •

The actor known for portraying the Marlboro Man in the iconic advertisements passed away from lung cancer.

• • •

In the 1960s, the CIA launched "Operation Acoustic Kitty," a project aiming to use cats for espionage, with listening devices implanted into them. The operation was ultimately deemed a failure due to the cats' indomitable will and instincts.

The banana slug, a North American species, is known for its enormous size and a mating ritual where sometimes the male's appendage gets stuck, leading the female to chew it off.

• • •

There's a whale called "52 Blue", often dubbed "the loneliest whale in the world", that sings at a unique frequency of 52 Hertz, unlike any other whale species, which has prevented it from communicating with other whales.

• • •

In 1983, an Air Canada Boeing 767 ran out of fuel mid-flight due to a miscalculation and had to glide to an emergency landing at an old airport that had been converted to a racetrack. It was nicknamed the "Gimli Glider".

The longest recorded flight of a paper airplane is 69.14 meters (226 feet, 10 inches), set by Joe Ayoob, a former NFL quarterback, and aircraft designer John Collins in 2012.

• • •

In 2006, a man set a record by wearing 257 T-shirts at the same time, ranging in size from small to 10XL.

• • •

The longest recorded flight of a chicken is 13 seconds. Despite having wings, chickens are not known for their flying abilities.

Sources

More People Died From Selfies Than Shark Attacks This Year, Report Says https://www.health.com/pain/selfie-shark-attack-deaths-mashable

Driscoll's Unveils the Top 10 Berry-Loving Markets in America https://www.businesswire.com/news/home/20170629005313/en/Driscoll%E2%80%99s-Unveils-Top-10-Berry-Loving-Markets-America

Myths of Human Genetics: Tongue Rolling https://udel.edu/~mcdonald/mythtongueroll.html

Ecommerce Trends in 2020 (+147 Statistics About Online Shopping) https://www.bigcommerce.com/blog/ecommerce-trends/

Tittle https://en.wikipedia.org/wiki/Tittle

Vanity sizing https://en.wikipedia.org/wiki/Vanity_sizing
member: Pope.L, 1978–2001 https://www.moma.org/calendar/exhibitions/5059

Here's the Science That Explains Why Drinking Diet Soda Makes You Gain Weight https://www.inc.com/minda-zetlin/diet-soda-weight-gain-metabolism-insulin-brain-fat-metabolic-syndrome.html

Double a Penny Every Day for 30 Days... Now Pay Taxes https://nomadcapitalist.com/2019/05/03/double-a-penny/

SOLUTION: what is the lowest number possible that when divided by 1, 2, 3, 4, 5, 6, 7, 8, 9, and 10 always has one left over, or a remainder of one? thanks a bunch. https://www.algebra.com/algebra/homework/word/numbers/Numbers_Word_Problems.faq.question.223183.html

Houdini's Promise to Prove Life After Death https://exemplore.com/paranormal/Houdinis-Promise

Infinity symbol https://en.wikipedia.org/wiki/Infinity_symbol

1***Is true that if the first of the month begins on a Sunday, the month will always have a Friday the 13th?*** https://www.quora.com/Is-true-that-if-the-first-of-the-month-begins-on-a-Sunday-the-month-will-always-have-a-Friday-the-13th

Can a person's ashes be turned into a diamond? https://www.heart-in-diamond.com/can-turn-person-ashes-diamonds.html

Why are 95% of people who live to 110 women? You're as old as your stem cells https://www.sciencedaily.com/releases/2015/06/150604141903.htm

Facts That Sounds Like They Are Not True - Crazy Trivia - What Was The First Thing Ever Bought On The Internet https://www.thrillist.com/culture/facts-that-sounds-like-they-are-not-true-crazy-trivia-what-was-the-first-thing-ever-bought-on-the-internet

McRib https://en.wikipedia.org/wiki/McRib

Karl Lagerfeld Dies With A Beautiful, Flawed Legacy https://www.refinery29.com/en-us/2019/02/224870/karl-lagerfeld-fashion-designer-legacy

Word Trivia - https://stevelaube.com/fun-fridays-word-trivia/

Iranians arrest 14 squirrels for spying https://www.ynetnews.com/articles/0,7340,L-3425130,00.html

How to find your way out of the woods without tools—or your phone https://www.popsci.com/navigate-without-tools-or-phone/

Get poo delivered to your enemy's door just in time for Christmas https://www.mirror.co.uk/news/weird-news/poo-delivered-your-enemys-door-4562728

Wearing Headphones For Just An Hour Can Increase Bacteria In Ears By 700 Times https://theproenzablog.com/featured/wearing-headphones-for-just-an-hour-can-increase-bacteria-in-ears-by-700-times/

8 Myths About Dead Bodies You Probably Think Are True https://www.mentalfloss.com/article/514257/8-myths-about-dead-bodies-you-probably-think-are-true

Taumatawhakatangihangakoauauotamateaturipukakapikimaunga-horonukupokaiwhenuakitanatahu https://en.wikipedia.org/wiki/Taumatawhakatangihangakoauauotamateaturipukakapikimaungahoronukupokaiwhenuakitanatahu

Return a Lost Driver's License By Dropping It In Any Mailbox https://lifehacker.com/return-a-lost-drivers-license-by-dropping-it-in-any-ma-510418965

Showering daily — is it necessary? - Harvard Health Blog https://www.health.harvard.edu/blog/showering-daily-is-it-necessary-2019062617193

How many birds are killed by windows? https://www.bbc.com/news/magazine-22395664

Here are a few of surfing's most high-profile lawsuits https://www.mensjournal.com/adventure/here-are-a-few-of-surfings-most-high-profile-lawsuits/

20 Statue of Liberty Facts | HowStuffWorks https://adventure.howstuffworks.com/20-facts-about-the-statue-of-liberty.htm

Female hurricanes are deadlier than male hurricanes https://www.pnas.org/content/111/24/8782

Measure Surface Tension with a Penny https://www.scientificamerican.com/article/measure-surface-tension-with-a-penny/

WATCH: What Happens When You Try to Fold Paper More Than 7 Times With a Hydraulic Press? https://www.sciencealert.com/watch-what-happens-when-you-try-to-fold-paper-more-than-7-times-with-a-hydraulic-press

Birthday problem https://en.wikipedia.org/wiki/Birthday_problem

The Cost of College Dropout https://www.thebalance.com/the-cost-of-college-dropout-4174303

Zoo realises it has been trying to mate two male hyenas for four years https://www.itv.com/news/2014-10-03/zoo-realises-it-has-been-trying-to-mate-two-male-hyenas-for-four-years/

Here's How Long It Really Takes to Break a Habit, According to Science https://www.sciencealert.com/how-long-it-takes-to-break-a-habit-according-to-science

Pogonophobia https://en.wikipedia.org/wiki/Pogonophobia

Mid-Day Naps Can Be a Sign of Bad Health https://www.smithsonianmag.com/smart-news/consistently-needing-take-long-mid-day-naps-might-be-indicative-underlying-health-problem-180951071/

Scholarships for Redhead 2020-2021 | USA Scholarships https://worldscholarshipforum.com/redhead-scholarship/

The Difference between Avocado and Lawyer in French https://www.livinglanguage.com/blog/2012/01/19/the-difference-between-avocado-and-lawyer-in-french/

Fact or Fiction?: Urinating on a Jellyfish Sting is an Effective Treatment https://www.scientificamerican.com/article/fact-or-fiction-urinating/

Open Cases: Why One-Third Of Murders In America Go Unresolved https://www.npr.org/2015/03/30/395069137/open-cases-why-one-third-of-murders-in-america-go-unresolved

Texas obscenity statute https://en.wikipedia.org/wiki/Texas_obscenity_statute

Wedding trends that did not exist before the 2010s https://www.insider.com/wedding-trends-that-did-not-exist-before-the-2010s-2019-12

A Californian Blind Man Uses Echolocation To Ride A Bike https://inhabitat.com/california-blind-man-uses-echolocation-to-navigate-around-on-his-bike/

Swedish man survived for two months in snowbound car thanks to 'igloo' effect https://www.telegraph.co.uk/news/worldnews/europe/sweden/9091674/Swedish-man-survived-for-two-months-in-snowbound-car-thanks-to-igloo-effect.html

"Can A Fine Whiskey Age Overnight?". 2021. *Nytimes.Com.* https://www.nytimes.com/2021/02/11/dining/drinks/whiskey-bespoken-lost-spirits.html.

"22 Things That Happened For The First Time In 2022". *2022.* Nytimes.Com. https://www.nytimes.com/2022/12/06/special-series/2022-firsts-year-in-review.html.

"Pink Barbie coffins: Funeral home in El Salvador takes Barbie mania to an extreme with new linings." *2023.* https://eu.usatoday.com/story/news/world/2023/08/08/funeral-home-el-salvador-selling-pink-coffins-with-barbie-linings/70555251007/

LeBLANC, S. *2023.* **"An extremely overdue book has been returned to a Massachusetts library 119 years later."** https://apnews.com/article/119-years-overdue-book-returned-fb615a7a32f654ad6981878d35376fc9

Gutoskey, E. *2022.* **"Chipotle Is Employing a Tortilla Chip-Making Robot Made Chippy, and Has Programmed It to Make Some Imperfect Chips."** https://www.mentalfloss.com/posts/chipotle-chip-robot

Cohen, L. *2023.* **""What the duck" is no more with Apple's new iPhone autocorrect update."** https://www.cbsnews.com/news/what-the-duck-apple-new-iphone-autocorrect-update-2023-worldwide-developers-conference/

Gutoskey, E. *2023.* **"One Scoop of the World's Most Expensive Ice Cream Will Set You Back Nearly $7000."** https://www.mentalfloss.com/posts/worlds-most-expensive-ice-cream

Welle, E. *2023.* **"World's first house made with nappy-blended concrete."** https://www.nature.com/articles/d41586-023-01701-x

"When the CIA Learned Cats Make Bad Spies." *(n.d).* https://www.history.com/news/cia-spy-cat-espionage-fail

Dolkas, M. *2021.* **"The Romantic Lives of Banana Slugs."** https://openspacetrust.org/blog/banana-slug/

Jamison, L. *2023.* **"52 Blue."** https://magazine.atavist.com/52-blue/

Staff, S. F. *2023.* **"The Incredible Story Of The Gimli Glider."** https://simpleflying.com/gimli-glider/

"Man wears 260 t-shirts simultaneously from medium to extra large, bags Guinness World Record." *(n.d.).* https://www.timesnownews.com/the-buzz/article/man-wears-260-t-shirts-simultaneously-from-medium-to-extra-large-bags-guinness-world-record/641358

Munson, O. *2023.* **"Did the chicken cross the road, or did it fly? Get to know more about the bird's flight."** https://eu.usatoday.com/story/news/2023/05/23/can-chickens-fly/70194618007/

ALSO BY JENNY KELLETT

... and more!

Available at

www.bellanovabooks.com

and all major online bookstores.

And that's all, folks!

I hope you enjoyed these facts and learned some interesting things to share with your family and friends.

I would very much appreciate your review—every review helps me to make bigger and better books next time!

If you'd like more fact books, visit: www.bellanovabooks.com

Printed in Great Britain
by Amazon

43913851R00260